THE KNITTER'S BIBLE knitted
homestyle

THE KNITTER'S BIBLE
knitted homestyle

David and Charles

www.rucraft.co.uk

A DAVID & CHARLES BOOK
Copyright © David & Charles Ltd 2009

David & Charles is an F+W Media Inc. company
4700 East Galbraith Road
Cincinnati, OH 45236

First published in the UK and USA in 2009

Text copyright © HACHETTE PARTWORKS LTD 2009

Photographs on pages 4, 8, 9, 10, 11, 12, 13, 104, 105, 108, 114 (top right
and bottom right), 116 (left), 118, 120, 121 (top left), 123 (top left, bottom left,
top middle and bottom middle), 125 and 126 copyright © David & Charles
Limited 2009

All other photographs copyright © HACHETTE PARTWORKS LTD 2009

Illustrations copyright © David & Charles Ltd 2009

A catalogue record for this book is available from the
British Library.

ISBN-13: 978-0-7153-3313-6 paperback
ISBN-10: 0-7153-3313-5 paperback

Printed in China by Shenzhen Donnelley Co Ltd
for David & Charles
Brunel House   Newton Abbot   Devon

Editor: Emily Rae
Assistant Editor: Kate Nicholson
Project Editor: Lorraine Slipper
Art Editor: Sarah Clark
Production Controller: Kelly Smith

Visit our website at www.davidandcharles.co.uk

David & Charles books are available from all good bookshops; alternatively you
can contact our Orderline on 0870 9908222 or write to us at FREEPOST EX2 110,
D&C Direct, Newton Abbot, TQ12 4ZZ (no stamp required UK only); US customers
call 800-289-0963 and Canadian customers call 800-840-5220.

contents

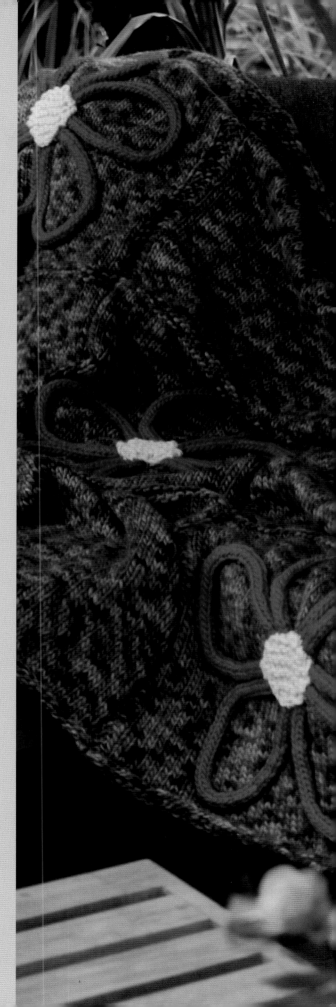

make your home special!

make your home special!

If you are a knitter and appreciate beautifully crafted handmade items, why not extend that appreciation to knitting for your home? It is an easy way to add a touch of opulence to your furnishings, or to ring the changes with new colours and textures to give your décor a lift. Why not knit accessories for every season so that you can change them to suit your mood? Knitted items for the home are also ideal gifts for someone special – they are often quick and easy to make and you don't have to worry about guessing the right size!

Most of the projects in this book require a basic knowledge of knitting, although full instructions for all of techniques used are given in the It's All About the Detail... section of the book. The projects provide opportunities to try out a mixture of techniques, some of which may be new to you, such as intarsia (Square Dance throw on page 42 and Daisy Pillow on page 74), Fair Isle (Shaker Hearts on page 50) and cables (Aran Throw on page 100). The more advanced techniques of knitting in the round on both circular and double-pointed needles are also used in various projects, such as the Funky Fruit Basket on page 22. and there is a chance to try your hand at fulling in the Bijou Boxes on page 30.

Some projects are quick and easy to make, such as the Super Chunky Throw on page 18, which uses thick yarn and large needles. Others will require more attention to detail, particularly in making up, to truly release their charm (see the delicious cakes in Tea-Time Treats on page 78 and the detailed vegetables on the Green Shopping Bag on page 58). Many of the

larger projects, such as the Paw-Print Dog Blanket on page 84, are knitted in strips, which are then sewn together. This means that you do not have to work with a large number of stitches on your needles at any time – and it also makes it easy to adjust the size of your blanket or throw by simply knitting as many extra strips as you need.

Many of the patterns, such as the Bull's-Eye Beanbag on page 26 and the Textured Table Runner on page 64, combine beauty with practicality. Other projects lend themselves to being purely decorative if you so wish – why not try knitting the Storage Pockets on page 94 as a wall hanging and fill the pockets with dried flowers or ornaments, rather than just using it to tidy up your things? All of the projects lend themselves to being knitted as gifts, but particularly the smaller ones such as the Scented Lavender Bags on page 54. Or if you know someone who is moving house, why not knit them a Breakfast Set (page 68) to help them relax the morning after?

Whatever reason you have to knit the patterns in this book, they will give you many hours of knitting pleasure and the inspiration to add something that is yours, especially to your home.

You can find instructions and diagrams for all the techniques used to make the projects in this book on pages 105 to 126. A comprehensive list of yarn spinners and suppliers around the world is given on page 127 to enable you to source the exact yarns you need.

Get knitting today and make your home truly special!

in the beginning . . .

fibres

Yarns have been chosen for the projects in this book bearing in mind whether they need to stand up to wear and cleaning – cotton and wool yarns are ideal here – or whether they are more decorative and can be worked in a softer fibre. For example, the Super Chunky Throw on page 18 could be made from a number of highly textured and decorative yarns available, whereas the Paw-Print Dog Blanket on page 84 is better made in a 100% synthetic yarn that can be thrown into the washing machine as required.

NATURAL FIBRES

Natural fibres can be made from either animal or plant sources. They often feel better than synthetic fibres and take dyes extremely well, so they can offer a better range of colours. However, they often need to be handled and washed with care, so you may prefer to choose synthetic fibres for items that need to stand up to heavy wear and frequent cleaning in the washing machine. Natural fibres are often more expensive than synthetic fibres, but they do add a touch of luxury and quality to any item.

Alpaca fleece makes a very fine and luxurious yarn. The alpaca is a member of the camel family and is a close relation of the llama. They are prized for their fleece as, unlike the llama, they are too small to be used as pack animals. Alpaca fleece is similar to sheep's wool but lighter in weight, silkier, warmer and with less lanolin. There are two types of alpaca: the Huacaya, which has dense, soft fleece with a crimped effect, and the Suri, which is more prized and has a longer, mop-like fleece. Alpaca has many of the qualities of cashmere but comes at a more affordable price.

Angora yarn consists of fibres taken from the coats of angora rabbits. The fur of these rabbits is soft and silky and yields a fibre that is fine with a fluffy 'halo'. Angora fibre is not very elastic, so it is often mixed with wool or synthetic fibres to make a more workable yarn. Items made from angora are beautifully soft and warm and will last for many years if looked after carefully.

Cashmere yarn comes from the downy undercoat of the Kashmir goat, and is plucked rather than shorn. Cashmere is notable because of the luxurious soft fibres that create a yarn that is lightweight, incredibly soft and very warm. This is the ultimate luxury yarn and 100% cashmere is very expensive. It is usually blended with other fibres, such as wool, to produce a soft yarn at a more reasonable price.

Cotton is produced from part of the seed case of the cotton bush. The fibres are short and have to be spun tightly together to make a uniform fibre. Mercerized cotton is boiled in lye (sodium hydroxide) to pre-shrink it and stop the fibres from becoming fuzzy. It has little elasticity and is often blended with other fibres to make it lighter. However, it lies flatter than wool and can be knitted up quite firmly, so it is often a suitable yarn for knitting items for the home. It is also long-lasting and hard-wearing and shows the texture of stitches to great effect.

Linen is part of the stem of the flax plant. It is processed several times to produce a finished fibre that is stiff and crunchy with little elasticity. It is often blended with cotton to soften it, but on its own it has a better drape than cotton.

Mohair comes from the angora goat and kid mohair comes from young goats of up to 18 months old. The long hairs make a yarn than can be brushed or unbrushed and that is light and airy. Although mohair may be knitted up on its own, it is often blended with other wools and fibres to give it strength.

Silk yarn is produced from the cocoons spun by silkworms, which are spun into a fine, strong yarn. Silk has a wonderful lustre and is soft with a dry feel.

Wool is generally used to refer to the fleece of a sheep, although technically all animal hair can be called wool. Different breeds of sheep produce different types of wool; for example, Shetland wool is harsher and more hard-wearing than Merino wool, as Shetland sheep live in the cold winters of the northern hemisphere, while Merino sheep are found in milder climates. Lambswool is the first shearing from an animal and is softer than subsequent shearings. Wool is a versatile yarn, being warm in winter and cool in summer. It knits up very well and stands up to unravelling and recycling with no loss of quality.

BLENDED AND SYNTHETIC FIBRES

Man-made yarns use substances that are not fibres originally but are made into fibres by the addition of chemicals. Synthetic yarns are durable and can be machine washed. They are often added to natural fibres to make a yarn that is cheaper and more elastic. Novelty yarns are often made from synthetic fibres. The most commonly used synthetic fibres are polyester, acrylic and polypropylene. Synthetic fibres also take dye well.

weight

The weight of a yarn is its thickness, and this is how yarns are classified. Pattern stitches can look very different when they are knitted in different weights of yarn; a thin, lightweight yarn will produce a soft and delicate fabric, whereas a thick, medium weight yarn will produce a thick, heavy fabric. Why not experiment for yourself with different yarn weights to see the effects that you can get?

PLY OR THICKNESS

A strand of spun yarn is called a single and plied yarn is created from singles twisted together, usually two, three or four plies. However, while the general rule is that the more plies twisted together, the thicker the yarn will be, this is not always the case because a ply could be large or small depending on the original fibre. The thickness of the yarn is also affected by the spinning process; a tightly spun ply will be thinner than a loosely spun ply. This can be seen if you compare a 2ply Shetland wool yarn which knits as a fine weight (4ply) yarn with a thick Lopi yarn (a traditional Icelandic wool yarn) which is formed of a single ply.

To add to the confusion, yarn manufacturers in the US and UK sometimes use different names for the same weight of yarn. Therefore the yarn requirements described in this book follow the standard developed by the Craft Yarn Council of America, which divides yarns into weights rather than numbers of plies, with the common UK equivalent given in brackets. Using the chart below, you should be able to find a suitable yarn for any of the projects in this book no matter where in the world you buy your yarn.

Super-bulky

Super-bulky

Bulky

Bulky

Bulky

Medium

Light

Light

Light

Fine

Fine

Super-fine

STANDARD YARN WEIGHTS

weight	gauge*	needle size**	yarn type***
super-fine	27–32 sts	1 to 3 (2.25–3.25mm)	sock, fingering (2ply, 3ply)
fine	23–26 sts	3 to 5 (3.25–3.75mm)	sport, baby (4ply)
light	21–24 sts	5 to 7 (3.75–4.5mm)	light worsted, DK (DK)
medium	16–20 sts	7 to 9 (4.5–5.5mm)	worsted, afghan (aran)
bulky	12–15 sts	9 to 11 (5.5–8mm)	chunky
super-bulky	6–11 sts	11 (8mm) and above	super-chunky

Notes: * Gauge (tension) is measured over 4in/10cm in stockinette (stocking) stitch
       ** US needle sizes are given first, with UK equivalents in brackets
       *** Alternative US yarn type names are given first, with UK equivalents in brackets

colour and texture

One of the most exciting things about knitting is the chance to experiment with colour. This gives every knitter the opportunity to put their own individual stamp on anything they knit. When knitting items for your home, you will want to choose colours that blend with your home décor, so don't be afraid to experiment with colour schemes other than the ones given in the patterns.

Using yarn with texture is also another way to put individual touches to a project. Yarns come in exciting forms such as bouclé, chenille, eyelash and ribbon, all of which have their own special characteristics. When knitting for the home, you may wish to stick to hard-wearing and easily washable yarns for practical reasons, but look out for the opportunity to use splashes of textured yarn to give pizzazz to your item.

Self-striping yarn has long lengths of colour that slowly merge into the next colour. To heighten the variegated effect, use two balls of yarn as you work, knitting two rows with one ball and the next two rows with the other. Or try working with one plain ball and one variegated ball.

Ribbon yarn is a woven version of tape that produces a flat yarn. It is available in many different fibres and can be multicoloured, stranded with other fibres, fluffy or crisp, slinky or hard.

Short-pile eyelash yarn resembles frayed ribbon. It can have short splashes of colour that merge through the texture of the yarn.

Tweed yarn is a marl of two or more colours punctuated with flecks of contrasting colours. Tweed yarn is great for fulling, producing a dense brushed fabric in which the colours merge.

Long-pile eyelash yarn knits up into a fabric of deep, shimmering waves with randomly placed colours. You can team it with a plain wool yarn to produce a striking effect.

Striped yarn is designed for smaller projects. In this example, each colour is separated by a dark blue stripe, so they are all clearly defined and do not merge with each other. Again, try using two balls at once, as with self-striping yarn, to break the sequence, or use two strands together to produce a marl yarn.

Self-striping yarn

Ribbon yarn

Short-pile eyelash yarn

Tweed yarn

Long-pile eyelash yarn

Striped yarn

Self-striping yarn (*shown twice 'cos it's so nice!*)

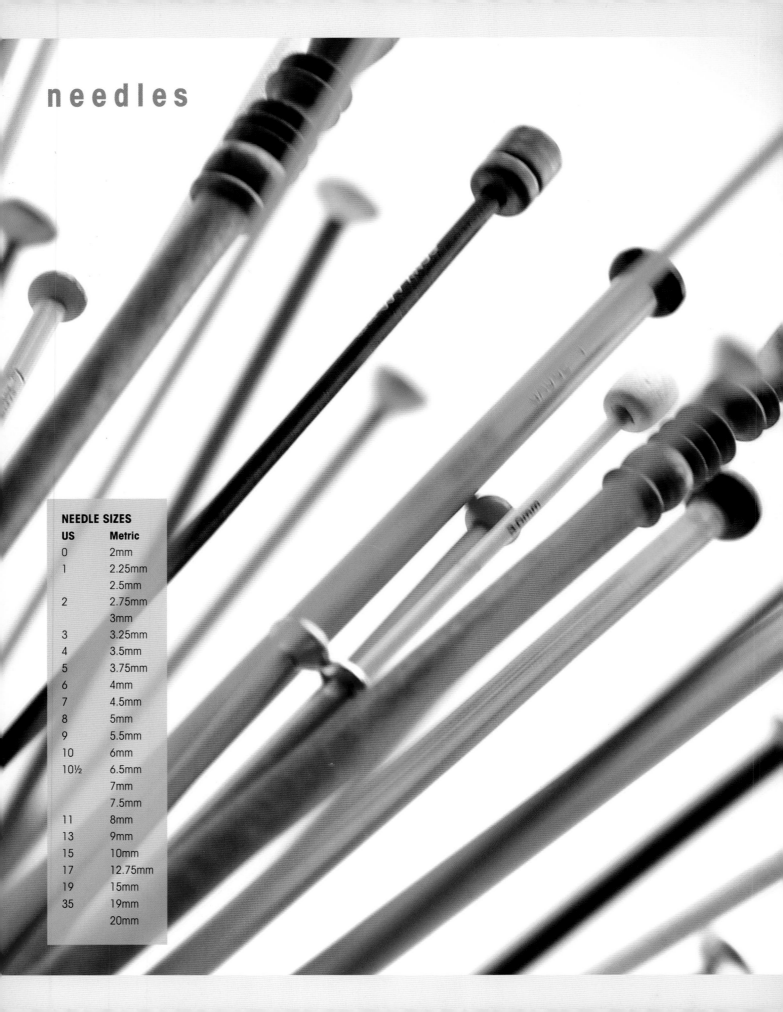

needles

NEEDLE SIZES

US	Metric
0	2mm
1	2.25mm
	2.5mm
2	2.75mm
	3mm
3	3.25mm
4	3.5mm
5	3.75mm
6	4mm
7	4.5mm
8	5mm
9	5.5mm
10	6mm
10½	6.5mm
	7mm
	7.5mm
11	8mm
13	9mm
15	10mm
17	12.75mm
19	15mm
35	19mm
	20mm

gauge (tension)

Gauge (tension) is the resistance on the yarn as it passes through your fingers as you knit. Keeping a moderate, consistent and correct tension will produce an even fabric. All patterns will specify the gauge (tension) that needs to be achieved to knit the project to the correct size. It is stated as the number of stitches and rows you need to make 4in (10cm) of fabric. It is important to take time to achieve the correct gauge (tension) before you start knitting your project.

GAUGE (TENSION) MEASUREMENT

To check your gauge (tension), work a square of fabric that measures at least 6in (15cm) using the stated yarn, needle size and stitch. This allows you to measure the fabric in the middle of the square, away from the edges which may be distorted.

You will not always be able to achieve both the correct stitch and row count. In these circumstances, it is more important to achieve the correct stitch count, as otherwise the item will be either too wide or not wide enough. Row count is less important as you can knit fewer or more rows to achieve the desired length if necessary. Row count becomes important when decrease instructions are given over an exact number of rows. If your row tension is not accurate, you may have to recalculate these decreases to ensure the item is the right length.

KNITTING A GAUGE (TENSION) SQUARE

Knit a gauge (tension) square in stockinette (stocking) stitch by casting on the number of stitches stated to measure 4in (10cm) plus half as many again.

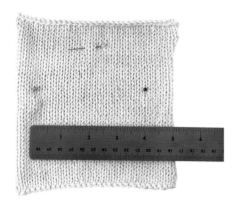

1 Work in stockinette (stocking) stitch for 6in (15cm) and bind (cast) off loosely.
2 Block the square in the same way that you will the finished item (see page 122).

3 Lay your square out on a flat surface without stretching it. Using a ruler, measure and mark with a pin 1in (2.5cm) in from one edge, and then 4in (10cm) from that pin.
4 For the rows, place the ruler vertically on the square and mark the same measurements, avoiding the cast-on and bound-off (cast-off) edges, which may pull the fabric in.
5 Count the number of stitches and rows between the pins to get your gauge (tension). If you have more stitches than the pattern states, your stitches are too small; try knitting the gauge (tension) square again with a size larger needle. If you have fewer stitches than the pattern states, your stitches are to big; try knitting the gauge (tension) square again with a size smaller needle.
6 Continue to adjust needle sizes and knit gauge (tension) squares until you achieve the gauge (tension) stated in the pattern.

MEASURING TEXTURED YARN

Yarn that has a lot of texture or long pile can be difficult to measure. Mark the measurements on long-pile yarns with long pieces of yarn in a contrasting colour. To make the stitches easier to see, try holding the fabric up to a window or a light. Take care to protect your eyes from strong light.

For textured yarn such as bouclé or chenille, knit sewing cotton in a contrasting colour in with the yarn as you make your square. This helps to show up the stitches. Again, mark the measurements with pieces of yarn in a contrasting colour instead of pins. This allows you to pull the fabric slightly to identify difficult stitches without the pins falling out.

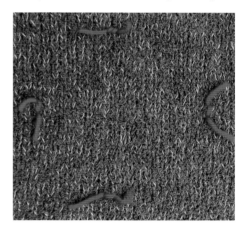

If you are still having difficulty, try counting the stitches on the reverse side of the fabric – for stockinette (stocking) stitch it is often easier to see the stitches on this side when using textured yarn.

MEASURING OVER A STITCH PATTERN

Where the gauge (tension) is given over a stitch pattern other than stockinette (stocking) stitch, cast on enough stitches to work complete repeats of the pattern. The repeat of the pattern is stated after the asterisk, so cast on a multiple of this number of stitches plus any stitches worked at the beginning and end of a row.

USING GAUGE (TENSION) FOR SUBSTITUTING YARNS

It is particularly important to check your gauge (tension) if using yarns other than those stated in the pattern, otherwise your finished item may be the wrong size. Instructions for working out how much yarn you will need are given on page 127.

abbreviations

All knitting patterns abbreviate instructions for the sake of brevity. This is a list of all the abbreviations used in the patterns in this book.

alt	alternate		**m**	metre(s)
BC	cable 2 to back		**m1**	make 1 stitch
beg	beginning		**mb**	make bobble ,
C3B	cable 3 to back		**mm**	millimetres
C3F	cable 3 to front		**oz**	ounces
C4	cable 4 to back		**p**	purl
C8B	cable 8 to back		**p2tog**	purl 2 together
C8F	cable 8 to front		**patt**	pattern
cm	centimetres		**psso**	pass slipped stitch over
cn	cable needle		**rem**	remaining
cont	continue		**rep**	repeat
dec	decrease		**RS**	right side
FC	cable 2 to front		**sl**	slip
foll	follows/following		**st st**	stockinette (stocking) stitch
g	gram(s)		**st(s)**	stitch(es)
g st	garter stitch		**tbl**	through back of loops
inc	increase		**tog**	together
in(s)	inch(es)		**WS**	wrong side
k	knit		**yd**	yards(s)
k1b	knit into back of stitch		**yfwd**	yarn forward
k2tog	knit 2 together		**yo**	yarn over needle to make a stitch
kfb	knit into front and back of stitch to make two stitches out of one		**yrn**	yarn round needle

Here is a list of the most common differences in US and UK knitting terms.

US TERM	UK TERM
stockinette stitch	stocking stitch
reverse stockinette stitch	reverse stocking stitch
seed stitch	moss stitch
moss stitch	double moss stitch
bind off	cast off
gauge	tension

reading knitting patterns

A knitting pattern is the instructions you need to make a project. For reasons of space, patterns use abbreviations and shorthand phrases. The abbreviations used in the patterns in this book are listed opposite. Many abbreviations, such as k and p, are used widely throughout all patterns. Other patterns may have specific abbreviations relating to specific stitches; these should always be explained in full at the beginning of the pattern.

WORKING FROM CHARTS

Patterns involving the intarsia or Fair Isle colourwork techniques are worked from charts. The pattern will usually give few other instructions, except to tell you how many stitches to cast on and instructions for any parts of the project not included in the chart. See page 113 for instructions on how to work from a chart. Instructions for any shaping required may be included in the chart as well as in the written instructions.

IMPERIAL AND METRIC MEASUREMENTS

The patterns give both imperial measurements (inches and ounces) and metric measurements (centimetres and grams). Make sure you stick to one set of measurements throughout your project; although most conversions are exact, there are some which are more generalized.

COMMON SHORTHAND PHRASES

Cont as set This is used to avoid repeating the same instructions over and over again. Just continue to work as previously instructed.

Keeping patt correct Again, to avoid repeating instructions, this tells you to ensure you work the pattern as previously instructed, even though you have been told to do something that would otherwise interfere with the pattern. For example, keeping centre panel pattern correct, cont in st st.

Work as given for This is where you are making two similar items. Instead of repeating the instructions in full as given for the first item, you are instructed to work the second item in the same way as the first item to a given point, which is usually marked by asterisks.

* Repeat instructions following an asterisk as many times as indicated or until you reach the end of a row.
** Double asterisks usually appear at the beginning and/or end of a section of instructions which will need to be repeated.
( ) Instructions in round brackets should be repeated the indicated number of times.

and now
to knit...

super chunky throw

Snuggle up with the ultimate mini-throw! With no shaping to worry about and using super-bulky (super-chunky) colourful yarn, you will soon be able to snuggle up with it. Bind the edges with a sheer ribbon in a matching colour and add a touch of glamour to your home.

Use a super-bulky (super-chunky) pure wool yarn to make your throw really cosy and comfy.

DESIGN SECRETS UNRAVELLED…

Why not experiment by using a mix of yarns to produce your own customized fabric? There are many yarns available with fantastic textures and colourways and you could combine two yarns – or even more, depending on their weight – to make your own totally original throw. For this project it is not vital to achieve the exact gauge (tension) stated, but be aware that any difference will affect the finished size of your throw. You can always cast on more or fewer stitches to adjust the size of your throw – but only if you take time to check your gauge (tension) before you start!

YARN FOCUS

The highly textured and super-bulky (super-chunky) yarn used for this throw is 100% pure wool. It knits up very quickly and there is a vast selection of variegated shades available in fantastic colour combinations that produce fabulous fabrics in even the most simple stitches.

super chunky throw

MEASUREMENTS

39in (100cm) wide and 43in (110cm) long

GATHER TOGETHER...
materials

9 × 3½oz (100g) hanks of super-bulky
(super-chunky) 100% wool yarn (54yd/50m
per hank) in a green mix shade

needles and notions

1 pair of size 17 (12.75mm) knitting needles
5yd (4.5m) of matching ribbon
Sewing needle and matching thread

GAUGE (TENSION)

7½sts and 10 rows measure 4in (10cm) square
over patt on size 17 (12mm) needles

Varying the sequence in which you work simple knit and purl rows gives an interesting and straightforward pattern. Here you work a knit row followed by a purl row, which gives two rows of stockinette (stocking) stitch, but this is followed by another purl row, which creates a garter stitch ridge, and then a knit row. This row sequence makes the pattern reversible.

knit your throw...

With size 17 (12.75mm) needles cast on 75 sts.
Row 1 K to end.
Row 2 P to end.
Row 3 P to end.
Row 4 K to end.
Rep these 4 rows to form patt until work measures 43in (109.5cm) from cast-on edge, ending with a 4th row. Bind (cast) off.

to finish...

Sew in all the loose ends of yarn. Lay the throw on a flat surface (possibly the floor), smooth out to the finished size and pin the edges if possible. Press with a warm iron over a slightly damp cloth.

sewing on ribbon

Fold ribbon in half lengthways and press to mark the crease line. Adding a ⅜in (1cm) seam allowance at each end, mark the corner points at 39in (100cm), 82in (210cm), 122in (310cm) and 165in (420cm). Taking ⅜in (1cm) seam allowance, sew ends of ribbon together to form a continuous loop. Pin the corner points in position at the appropriate corners, sandwiching the knitting between the two layers of folded ribbon. Pin free edge of ribbon in place along all four sides. At each corner work a line of small gathering stitches along each free inner edge. Draw up the gathering stitches so that ribbon fits round corner and pin in place. Repeat on the other side. Using small running stitch and matching sewing thread, stitch ribbon in place along inner edge, working through all three layers and repeat on the other side of the throw.

funky fruit basket

Store your fruit in this fun basket. It is worked in the round on a circular needle (see page 116) in a colourful variegated wool and then fulled in the washing machine. This is a sure-fire way to give your home that truly tropical look.

The bright colours of this basket make it both practical and pretty.

(see page 116)

DESIGN SECRETS UNRAVELLED…

The variegated yarn used to make this fruit basket is guaranteed to give a tropical zing to your home. For a more understated look, choose a solid shade in earthy brown or terracotta to tone in with your furniture. Or add a personal touch by using two different yarns together – make sure they are both 100% pure wool to ensure they will full.

YARN FOCUS

The 100% pure wool yarn used in this project has a soft, loose construction that is ideal for fulling. There are plenty of shades to choose from, including a few variegated ones. Two strands are used together to produce a sturdy yet sumptuous fabric.

funky fruit basket

MEASUREMENTS
Approximately 13½in (35cm) wide and
3½in (9cm) deep after fulling

GATHER TOGETHER...
materials
9 × 1½oz (50g) balls of super-bulky
(super-chunky) 100% pure wool yarn (54yd/50m
per ball) in autumn shades

needles and notions
1 pair size 15 (10mm) circular knitting needle
Set of size 15 (10mm) double-pointed
knitting needles
Stitch markers

GAUGE (TENSION)
Before fulling: 10 sts and 13 rows measure
4in (10cm) square over st st on size 15 (10mm)
needles using 2 strands of yarn together

knit note: *work with 2 strands of yarn together throughout. Make sure that you work through both strands for every stitch.*

knit note: *when working in rounds, you knit every row to produce stockinette (stocking) stitch, as you never have to turn the work.*

Starting at the rim, use a circular needle to work in rounds using two ends of yarn throughout. Work in rounds of stockinette (stocking) stitch (knit every round), shaping with simple decreases. As the number of stitches get smaller, change to double-pointed needles. Follow instructions to full the finished bowl in a washing machine on page 118. Remember – fulling is not an exact science!

knit your fruit basket...
With size 15 (10mm) circular needle and 2 strands of yarn, cast on 120 sts. Cont in rounds, work as foll: (k 1 round and p 1 round) twice. Now cont in st st (k every round) throughout, work 18 rounds.
Next round *K30, place marker, rep from * to end.
Next round *K to 2 sts before marker, k2tog, rep from * to end. 116 sts.
Cont to dec 4 sts in this way on every round until 8 sts rem and changing to double-pointed needles when necessary.
Next round *K2tog, rep from * to end. 4 sts.
Cut off yarn, thread through rem sts, draw up and fasten off.

to finish...
Full the bowl by washing in a machine at 60 degrees, placing a few towels in the load as well for extra agitation. Reshape bowl while still damp and stuff with crumpled balls of newspaper. Place heavy books on top of newspaper stuffing and leave to dry. Remove paper and allow bowl to dry thoroughly.

bull's-eye beanbag

Worked in a super-bulky (super-chunky) yarn on large needles using easy stitches, you can rustle up this beanbag in no time at all. This is the perfect eye-catching accessory for when it's time to put your feet up and relax … and, of course, do some more knitting!

Practise your circular knitting skills on this striking and practical addition to your home.

bull's-eye beanbag

Using easy stitches and simple increases, this is a good project for someone new to circular knitting. Take care when assembling your beanbag to achieve a neat finish.

MEASUREMENTS

Finished beanbag measures 23½in (60cm) in diameter and 11in (28cm) high

GATHER TOGETHER...

materials

Super-bulky (super-chunky) acrylic/cotton/wool mix yarn (82yd/75m per 3½oz (100g) ball):

A 5 balls in denim blue
B 3 balls in ivory

needles and notions

Size 15 (10mm) circular knitting needles in 16in (40cm), 32in (80cm) and 40in (100cm) lengths
1 pair of size 15 (10mm) knitting needles
Size K-10½ (7mm) crochet hook
2yd (2m) canvas
3½ cubic feet (0.1 cubic metres) polystyrene beads

GAUGE (TENSION)

8 sts and 12 rows measure 4in (10cm) square over st st on size 15 (10mm) needles

knit your beanbag...

circular panels (make 2)

With 16in (40cm)-long circular needle and A, cast on 4 sts. Work in rows as foll:

1st and foll alt rows P to end.
2nd row K into front, back and front of each st. 12 sts.
4th row K to end, inc in each st. 24 sts.
Change to B.
6th row *K1, inc in next st, rep from * to last 2 sts, k2. 35 sts.
8th row *K2, inc in next st, rep from * to last 2 sts, k2. 46 sts.
Now start working in rounds as foll:
1st round K to end.
2nd round *K3, inc in next st, rep from * to last 2 sts, k2. 57 sts.
Change to A.
3rd and 4th rounds K to end.
5th round *K4, inc in next st, rep from * to last 2 sts, k2. 68 sts.
6th and 7th rounds K to end.
Change to 32in (80cm)-long circular needle.
8th round *K5, inc in next st, rep from * to last 2 sts, k2. 79 sts.
9th round K to end.
Change to B.
10th and 11th rounds K to end.
12th round *K6, inc in next st, rep from * to last 2 sts, k2. 90 sts.
13th–15th rounds K to end.
Change to A.

16th round *K7, inc in next st, rep from * to last 2 sts, k2. 101 sts.
17th–20th rounds K to end.
21st round *K8, inc in next st, rep from * to last 2 sts, k2. 112 sts.
Change to 40in (100cm)-long circular needle.
22nd round K to end.
Change to B.
23rd and 24th rounds K to end.
25th round *K9, inc in next st, rep from * to last 2 sts, k2. 123 sts.
26th and 27th rounds K to end.
Change to A.
28th round K to end.
29th round *K10, inc in next st, rep from * to last 2 sts, k2. 134 sts.
30th round K to end.
Bind (cast) off loosely.

side panel

With size 15 (10mm) needles and A, cast on 22 sts. Beg on WS, p 3 rows. Join in B. Cont in stripe patt.
1st and 2nd rows With B, k to end.
3rd row With A, k to end.
4th–6th rows With A, p to end.
The last 6 rows form stripe patt. Rep them until panel measures 74in (188cm) from beg, when slightly stretched, ending with a 4th patt row. Bind (cast) off.

to finish...

Using circular panel as a template and allowing ½in (2cm) extra seam allowance all round, cut two circles from canvas. Also cut a 75 × 12in (192 × 31cm) rectangle from canvas. With RS facing and raw edges matching, join short ends of rectangle to form an open circle.

Now sew one edge of open circle around one circular panel. Sew remaining edge of open circle to other circular panel, leaving a gap for turning through. Turn to RS and fill with polystyrene beads.

Slipstitch opening firmly closed. Join cast-on and bound-off (cast-off) edges of side panel to form an open circle. Using mattress stitch, sew row ends of circular panels together in centre. Place all pieces over beanbag and pin together at edges with WS facing. With size K-10½ (7mm) hook and A, crochet seams together with double crochet.

bijou boxes

Combine knitting, fulling and sewing to great effect with these fabulous fulled boxes. After fulling the knitted pieces are cut to shape and sewn together, and then decorated with flower motifs and cross stitch embroidery. Like the famous matryoshka (Russian stacking dolls), these boxes fit neatly inside each other when empty. Ideal for storing jewellery, these delightful boxes would make a glamorous addition to any boudoir.

These elegant little boxes would make an ideal gift for a special person – or perhaps you will love them so much that you won't be able to give them away.

YARN FOCUS

The super-bulky (super-chunky) weight 100% wool yarn that is used is very soft and has a loose construction, making it ideal for fulling. A good range of colours is available, including some variegated shades and the resulting fabric can be cut and sewn.

DESIGN SECRETS UNRAVELLED…

You can personalize the boxes to suit your own décor by adding buttons, beads and sequins to give them some glitz. Try replacing the fulled petals with shop-bought trims of beautiful fabric flowers or exotic feathers. The possibilities are endless!

bijou boxes

MEASUREMENTS

Box 1 (cream with claret flower): 8⅝in (22cm) in
diameter and 5in (13cm) high

Box 2 (claret with cream flower): 8⅝in (22cm) in
diameter and 4¼in (11cm) high

Box 3 (small claret with cream flower):
5½in (14cm) in diameter and 3⅛in (8cm) high

Box 4 (all sky blue with cream flower):
3½in (9cm) in diameter and 2¾in (7cm) high

GATHER TOGETHER...
materials

Super-bulky (super-chunky) 100% pure wool yarn
(54yd/50m per 1¾oz (50g) ball):

A 11 balls in claret

B 9 balls in cream

C 2 balls in sky blue

needles and notions

1 pair of size 15 (10mm) knitting needles

Tapestry needle

Matching sewing thread and needle

GAUGE (TENSION)

10 sts and 14 rows measure 4in (10cm)
square over st st on size 15 (10mm) needles
before fulling

The boxes are formed from fabric pieces made in simple stockinette (stocking) stitch, so should take no time at all to knit. But make sure that you take time and care over the fulling and assembly to ensure that your boxes achieve their potential.

knit your boxes...
boxes 1 and 2 (make 1 in claret and 1 in cream)
body

With size 15 (10mm) needles cast on 30 sts. Work in st st until strip measures 47in (120cm). Bind (cast) off.

circles (make 2 in each of claret and cream for lids and box bases)

With size 15 (10mm) needles cast on 15 sts. Beg with a k row, cont in st st, inc 1 st at each end of every foll alt row until there are 45 sts. Work straight to 12in (30cm) from beg, ending with a p row. Dec 1 st at each end of next and every foll alt row until 15 sts rem. Work 1 row.
Bind (cast) off.

box 3
body

With size 15 (10mm) needles and claret, cast on 22 sts. Work in st st until strip measures 25½in (65cm). Bind (cast) off.

lid and base circles (make 2)

With size 15 (10mm) needles and claret, cast on 7 sts. Beg with a k row, cont in st st, inc 1 st at each end of every foll alt row until there are 21 sts. Work straight to 5½in (14cm) from beg, ending with a p row. Dec 1 st at each end of next and every foll alt row until 7 sts rem. Work 1 row. Bind (cast) off.

box 4
body

With size 15 (10mm) needles and turquoise, cast on 15 sts. Work in st st until strip measures 20in (50cm). Bind (cast) off.

lid and base circles (make 2)

With size 15 (10mm) needles and turquoise, cast on 5 sts. Beg with a k row, cont in st st, inc 1 st at each end of every foll alt row until there are 15 sts. Work straight to 4in (10cm) from beg, ending with a p row. Dec 1 st at each end of next and every foll alt row until 5 sts rem. Work 1 row. Bind (cast) off.

to finish...

Full pieces by washing at 60 degrees in a machine with a few towels or pairs of jeans for extra agitation. Reshape while still damp and dry flat. Press flat while still slightly damp or after spraying with water. When completely dry, cut pieces to the following dimensions, saving any off-cuts for petals:

boxes 1 and 2
lids and bases

8½in (21cm) diameter circles
From each full length body strip, cut the following pieces:
cream: 4½in (12cm) wide base strip and 1⅛in (3cm) wide lid strip
claret: 4in (10cm) wide base strip and 1⅛in (3cm) wide lid strip.

box 3
lid and base

5in (13cm) diameter circle
From full length body strip, cut the following pieces:
2½in (7cm) wide base strip and 1½in (4cm) wide lid strip.

box 4
lid and base

3⅛in (8cm) diameter circles
From full length body strip, cut the following pieces:
2⅜in (6cm) wide base strip and 1⅛in (3cm) wide lid strip.

Now join lid strip to lid circle by positioning raw edge of strip around outer edge of circle (to make the lid larger than the base) and, using matching sewing thread, sew small, neat zigzag stitches through the felt fabric (there will be small stitches visible on the outer surfaces). Trim the strip to size and join the two ends of strip. Repeat this process to join the base strip to the base circle, placing the raw edge of strip on top of circle (to make box smaller than lid).

Cut five flower petals for each box with lengths of 3½in (9cm) for box 1, 3⅛in (8cm) for box 2, 2⅜in (6cm) for box 3 and 1½in (4cm) for box 4. Arrange the petals so that the points meet in the centre of the lid. Attach each petal with a few stitches through the central tip so that the outer tips can curl upwards slightly. Using yarn in a contrasting colour and a tapestry needle, sew large cross stitches across the joins on the box and lid as shown. Finally, spray finished box with water, pack with crumpled newspaper then leave to dry to help the boxes maintain their shape.

summer garland

Celebrate in style with this gorgeous garland. Mounted on satin ribbon, the pennants are knitted in a variety of patterns using delicious ice-cream colours and backed with printed fabric. Combine them with the Tea-Time Treats pattern and create your very own afternoon tea party under the trees.

The practical 100% cotton yarns means these pennants can easily be used both inside and outside the house.

YARN FOCUS

The 100% cotton yarn used in this project is softly spun with a light sheen that produces good-looking fabrics. There are plenty of colours to choose from, including some strong shades as well as pretty pastels.

DESIGN SECRETS UNRAVELLED...

Because they are individually a small project, these pennants lend themselves to experimentation. Try making up your own versions of the stripe, spot and check patterns and create your own intarsia motif. Experiment with embellishments such as embroidery, buttons, sequins and beads. Knit the pennants in colours to coordinate with the colour theme of a garden wedding and use them to enhance the decorations. Or knit them in the colours of your favourite football team and show your support!

summer garland

The patterns on the pennants are achieved by a combination of techniques,
including intarsia (see page 112), Fair Isle (see page 114) and Swiss darning
(see page 119). Their small scale makes them an ideal project for anyone
wanting to try out a new technique before committing to a larger project.

knit your garland...
basic pennant

With size 6 (4mm) needles and yarn specified
for each pennant, cast on 33 sts. Work in st st
throughout, shaping as foll:

1st row (RS) K to end.

2nd row P to end.

3rd row K1, sl 1, k1, psso, k to last 3 sts, k2tog, k1.

4th row P to end.

5th row As 3rd row.

6th row P to end.

Rep last 6 rows 3 times more. 17 sts.

Next row K to end.

Next row P to end.

Next row K1, sl 1, k1, psso, k to last 3 sts, k2tog, k1.

Next row P to end.

Rep last 4 rows twice more. 11 sts.

Next row K1, sl 1, k1, psso, k to last 3 sts, k2tog,
k1. 9 sts.

Beg with a p row, work 3 rows in st st.

Next row K1, sl 1, k1, psso, k to last 3 sts, k2tog, k1.

Next row P to end.

Rep last 2 rows once more. 5 sts. Work 2 rows in
st st.

Next row: K1, sl 1, k1, psso, k2tog.

Next row: P3tog and fasten off.

striped pennant (make 2)

Foll instructions for Basic Pennant, cast on using A
and cont working throughout in stripes of 2 rows
each A, B, A and C.

heart motif pennant (make 2)

With D, cast on and work first 6 rows of Basic
Pennant. Using intarsia method (using small
separate balls of yarn for each area of colour and
twisting yarns tog on WS of work when changing
colour), cont to shape as set, placing Chart 1 on
7th row as foll: K8 D, k across 13 sts of 1st row of
Chart 1, k8 D. Reading odd-numbered (RS) rows
from right to left and even-numbered (WS) rows
from left to right and cont to dec as set, work until
21 rows from chart have been completed. Cut off B
and E and complete pennant with D only.

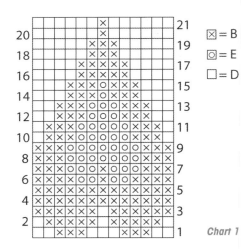

⊠ = B

◎ = E

☐ = D

Chart 1

checked pennant (make 2)

Foll instructions for Basic Pennant, cast on using B. K 1 row, then beg with a p row cont working throughout in stripes of 4 rows B and 1 row C. Afterwards, foll Chart 2, Swiss darn vertical stripes in D and E as indicated.

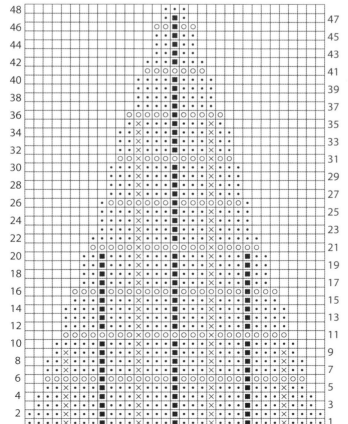

⊡ = B
⊙ = C
■ = D
⊠ = E

Chart 2   37

spotted pennant (make 2)

With C, cast on and work first 2 rows of Basic Pennant. Using Fair Isle method (stranding yarn not in use across WS of work), cont to shape as set, placing Chart 3 on 3rd row as foll: K1, sl 1, k1, psso, k across 27 sts of 1st row of Chart 3, k2tog, k1. Reading odd-numbered (RS) rows from right to left and even-numbered (WS) rows from left to right and cont to dec as set, work until 42 rows from chart have been completed. Cut off A and E and complete pennant with C only.

to finish...

Press according to directions on ball band. Lay each pennant on to chosen fabric and cut out fabric, adding ⅝in (1.5cm) turnings all round. Press under turnings on fabric and with WS facing, slipstitch fabric backing to pennants. Take the length of ribbon and lay first pennant on top, 23½in (60cm) from one end, with top edge of pennant level with top edge of ribbon. Neatly sew the ribbon to the top and sides of pennant. Leave a 2in (5cm) gap and, following order shown in photograph, continue to position and sew pennants on to ribbon. Trim ribbon at end of bunting to 23½in (60cm) to match first end.

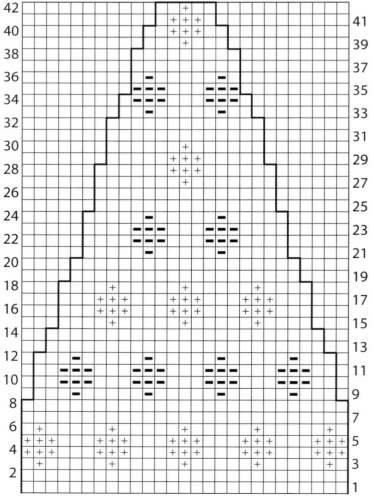

■ = A

⊞ = E

☐ = C

Chart 3

op art options

Create an optical illusion with a dramatic
black and white throw based on a
design of squares within squares. Team
it with a stunning pillow/cushion with
a clever geometric triangle pattern
– the black and white colour scheme
increases the optical illusion created
by the four squares. Both projects use
simple stockinette (stocking) stitch,
garter stitch and the intarsia method
(see page 112).

*The geometric patterns are set off
beautifully with a two-tone garter
stitch border.*

YARN FOCUS

Add some luxury to your home with
this yarn that combines of 60% silk,
20% rayon and 20% cotton. The silk
content gives the yarn a subtle sheen
and drape, but it can still be washed at
low temperatures. There is a fabulous
shade range to choose from for other
graphic colourways.

square dance

MEASUREMENTS

Finished throw measures 47in (120cm) wide and 59in (150cm) long

GATHER TOGETHER...
materials

Medium weight (aran) silk/rayon/cotton mix yarn (96yd/88m per 1½oz (50g) ball):

A 16 balls in black
B 15 balls in white

needles

1 pair of size 8 (5mm) knitting needles
1 size 8 (5mm) circular knitting needle, 32in (80cm) or 40in (100cm) long

GAUGE (TENSION)

16.5 sts and 24.5 rows measure 4in (10cm) square over chart patt on size 8 (5mm) needles

The striking combination of squares in just two colours with the colours reversed each time makes a very graphic pattern for this contemporary throw. Worked in stockinette (stocking) stitch, it has a striped garter-stitch edging. Take care working the edging to achieve a truly professional look.

knit your throw...

1st row, square 1 With size 8 (5mm) needles and A, cast on 26 sts. Beg with a k row, cont in st st and patt from chart, reading odd-numbered (k) rows from right to left and even-numbered (p) rows from left to right. Over centre 26 rows, use small separate balls of yarn for each area of colour, twisting yarns tog on WS of work when changing colour. When 38 rows have been completed, bind (cast) off.

square 2 With size 8 (5mm) needles, B and RS of Square 1 facing, pick up and k 26 sts along bound-off (cast-off) edge of square 1. Work as given for Square 1, reversing the colours.

Cont in this way until there are 9 squares in 1st row. Make 6 more rows of squares, reversing the colours each time as shown in the diagram.

to finish...

Press rows of squares according to directions on ball band. Using mattress stitch, join rows together as shown in diagram to form throw.

side edgings

With size 8 (5mm) circular needle, A and RS of throw facing, pick up and k 172 sts along one long edge. *Working forwards and backwards in rows, k 1 row. Cont in g st and stripes as foll: (2 rows B and 2 rows A) 3 times, 2 rows B and 1 row A. Bind (cast) off knitwise on WS with A.*
Rep edging on other long edge of throw.

top and bottom edgings

With size 8 (5mm) circular needle, A and RS of throw facing, pick up and k 9 sts across end of side edging, then 175 sts along top edge of throw (picking up 25 sts from bound-off (cast-off) edge of each square) and 9 sts across end of other side edging. 193 sts. Work as given for side edging from * to *.
Rep edging on bottom edge of throw.

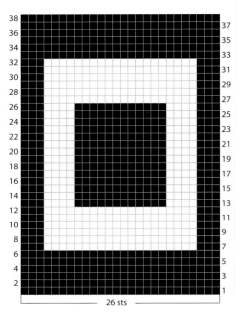

26 sts

1st row   2nd row

triangulation

MEASUREMENTS

Pillow/cushion measures 16in (40cm) square

GATHER TOGETHER...
materials

1 × 14oz (400g) ball of medium weight (aran)
acrylic/wool mix yarn (96yd/88m per ball) in each
of the following colours:

A black
B white

needles and notions

1 pair of size 7 (4.5mm) knitting needles
16in (40cm) square cushion pad

GAUGE (TENSION)

19 sts and 24 rows measure 4in (10cm) square
over st st on size 7 (4.5mm) needles

YARN FOCUS

This medium weight (aran) yarn with an acrylic/
wool mix is so practical for home furnishings.
It can be machine-washed on a wool programme
and there are plenty of shades to choose for
two-colour geometric combinations.

Create an optical illusion with this striking black and white pillow/cushion featuring a geometric pattern. The four squares forming the front are all the same – it's their arrangement that counts!

knit your pillow/cushion...
front
square (make 4)

With size 7 (4.5mm) needles and A, cast on 39 sts.
Beg with a k row, cont in st st and patt from chart.
Read odd-numbered (k) rows from right to left and
even-numbered (p) rows from left to right. Use
small, separate balls of yarn for each area of colour
and twist yarns tog on WS of work when changing
colours to avoid holes forming. Work 49 rows from
chart. Bind (cast) off.

back

With size 7 (4.5mm) needles and A, cast on 71 sts.
Beg with a k row, cont in st st until work measures
16in (40cm) from beg, ending with a p row. Bind
(cast) off.

to finish...

Press pieces carefully according to directions on
ball band. Join the four squares together to form
the cushion front, matching black to white edges
as shown in the picture. With RS facing, join back to
front by backstitching around three sides. Turn work
to RS. Insert cushion pad and use mattress stitch to
close the fourth side.

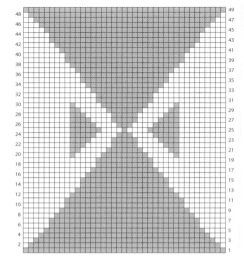

folk art pillow

Worked in stockinette (stocking) stitch with a reverse stockinette (stocking) stitch back, the colours and simple stylized floral pattern of this pillow/cushion are reminiscent of folk art. Traditional colours and embroidered motifs give this pillow/cushion a homely, folksy appeal. Curving lines of stems and leaves are embroidered on afterwards.

The embroidered stems add interest and texture to this charming heirloom.

DESIGN SECRETS UNRAVELLED...

The colours of this pillow/cushion conjure up a feeling of nostalgia and tradition. It would look equally authentic in a palette of neutral browns and creams, echoing the undyed colour of sheep fleece. Either way, you can create your own personal heirloom to treasure.

YARN FOCUS

This 100% merino wool in a softly spun, chunky construction has a slightly felted appearance. It can be hand-washed and there is a small range of solid colours to choose from.

folk art pillow

MEASUREMENTS
Finished pillow/cushion measures
15in (38cm) square

GATHER TOGETHER...
materials
Medium weight (aran) 100% merino wool
(77yd/70m per 1½oz (50g) ball):
A 4 balls in denim blue
B 1 ball in cherry red

needles and notions
1 pair of size 8 (5mm) knitting needles
1 × 11yd (10m) skein of tapestry wool in green
Blunt-ended wool needle
16in (40cm) square cushion pad

GAUGE (TENSION)
17 sts and 21 rows measure 4in (10cm) square
over st st on size 8 (5mm) needles

knit note: work motifs on Front in B using the intarsia technique (see page 112) with a separate small ball of yarn (or wind yarn on to bobbins) for each one. Twist yarns tog at edges of motifs when changing colours to prevent holes forming. When working motifs, strand or weave colour A across the WS of the work (see page 114).

This is a good project for practising your intarsia technique as there is no shaping to worry about. The back is knitted in one colour so that you do not have to worry about forming the opening while following the intarsia pattern.

knit your pillow/cushion...
front
With size 7 (5mm) needles and A, cast on 65 sts.
Beg with a k row, cont in st st and work 10 rows. Join in B. Cont in st st, work in patt from chart as foll:
1st row (RS) K7 B, k across 30 sts of 1st row of chart reading from right to left, then rep 21 motif sts again reading from left to right, k7 B.
2nd row P7 B, p across 21 motif sts of 2nd row of chart, reading from right to left, then p across 30 sts of 2nd row of chart reading from left to right, p7 B.
Cont in patt as set from chart until 61 rows have been completed. Cut off B. Cont in A, work 10 more rows, ending with a RS row. Bind (cast) off.

back panels
top section
With size 7 (5mm) needles and A, cast on 65 sts.
Beg with a p row, cont in reverse st st until work measures 9in (23cm) from beg, ending with a k row. Work opening edge as foll:
Next row (RS) K to end.
Next row K1, (p1, k1) to end.
Next row K to end.
Next row P1, (k1, p1) to end.
Rep last 4 rows twice more. Bind (cast) off.

bottom section
Work as given for top section until work measures 7in (18cm) from beg, ending with a k row. Work 2 rows as given for opening edge of top section. Bind (cast) off.

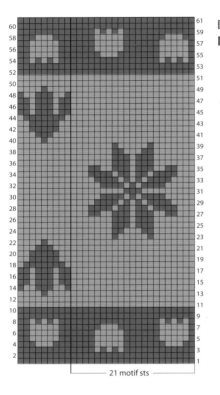

= A
= B

21 motif sts

to finish...
Press according to directions on ball band. Using green tapestry wool, embroider chain stitch lines as shown in the picture. Keep the chain stitches fairly large and even. Work leaves (groups of three lazy daisy stitches) at intervals as shown.

Lay the cushion front with right side facing up. Place the top section then bottom section of back panels on top, with right sides facing down and overlapping opening edges in the centre. Join together by backstitching around outer edges. Turn right side out through back opening. Insert cushion pad.

shaker hearts

This collection of stockinette (stocking) stitch hearts with decorative colourwork and embroidery is just right to hang in your home. They would make the perfect present for a new homeowner, and they are quick and easy to knit too.

These pretty hearts would make the perfect gift for someone special in your life.

DESIGN SECRETS UNRAVELLED...
Although red, pink and white are the obvious colour choices for a set of hearts, they would look equally appealing in blue and white. These hearts also lend themselves to decoration with ribbon, sequins and other trimmings in addition to buttons. So, let your imagination run riot and you will soon have your heart's desire.

YARN FOCUS
The hearts are made in a practical mixture of 55% wool, 25% acrylic and 20% nylon. There is a comprehensive shade range giving you plenty of choice for colourwork.

shaker hearts

MEASUREMENTS

Each finished heart is approximately 4½in (11cm)
wide and 5in (13cm) long

GATHER TOGETHER...
materials

1 × 1½oz (50g) ball of lightweight (DK) wool/
acrylic/nylon mix yarn (131yd/120m per ball)
in each of the following colours:

A red

B pink

C white

needles and notions

1 pair of size 6 (4mm) knitting needles

Polyester toy stuffing

5 small white buttons

1 large white button

30in (75cm) of narrow red satin ribbon

Sewing needle and thread

GAUGE (TENSION)

22 sts and 28 rows measure 4in (10cm) square
over st st on size 6 (4mm) needles

The red heart is easy to make, but the pink and white hearts involve a little work from charts using Fair Isle and intarsia techniques (see pages 112–114).

knit your hearts...
red heart
back

With size 6 (4mm) needles and A, cast on 3 sts.
Cont in st st and shape as foll:

1st row P to end.

Next row (RS) K1, (yfwd, k1) twice. 5 sts.

Next row P1, yrn, p into back of loop made on previous row, p1, p into back of loop made on previous row, yrn, p1. 7 sts.

Next row K1, yfwd, k into back of loop made on previous row, k to last 2 sts, k into back of loop made on previous row, yfwd, k1.

Next row P1, yrn, p into back of loop made on previous row, p to last 2 sts, p into back of loop made on previous row, yrn, p1.

Rep last 2 rows until there are 31 sts. Work 19 rows straight, ending with a k row.

shape top

Next row P16, turn and cont on these sts only.

Next row Bind (cast) off 1 st, k to last 2 sts, k2tog. 14 sts.

Dec 1 st at each end of next 4 rows. Bind (cast) off rem 6 sts.

With WS facing, rejoin yarn to rem 15 sts and p to end. Dec 1 st at beg of next row. 14 sts. Dec 1 st at each end of next 4 rows. Bind (cast) off rem 6 sts.

front

Work as given for Back.

to finish...

With C and following Chart 1, work cross-stitch heart motif in centre of front and individual cross stitches for border. Cut a 10in (25cm) length of ribbon and fold in half to form a loop. With matching sewing thread stitch raw edges of ribbon loop securely to WS of top of front heart. With RS facing, backstitch around front and back, leaving a small opening in one side. Turn to RS through opening, stuff lightly and close opening.

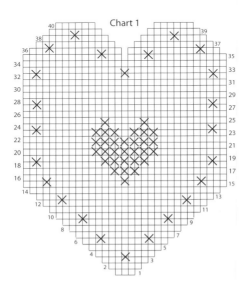

Chart 1

white heart

back

With C, work as given for Red Heart.

front

With C, work as given for back, placing small squares patt as shown on Chart 2. Use small,

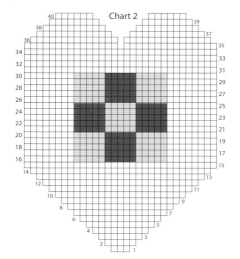

Chart 2

separate balls of C at either side of small squares patt, twisting yarns tog on WS of work when changing colours to avoid holes forming and strand A and B loosely across WS of work.

to finish...

Sew a small white button to centre of each pink square. Cut a 10in (25cm) length of ribbon and fold in half to form a loop. With matching sewing thread stitch raw edges of ribbon loop securely to WS of top of front heart. With RS facing, backstitch around front and back, leaving a small opening in one side. Turn to RS through opening, stuff lightly and close opening.

pink heart

back

With B, work as given for Red Heart.

front

With B, work as given for back, placing gingham patt as shown on Chart 3. Strand colours not in use loosely across WS of work.

to finish...

Cut a 10in (25cm) length of ribbon and fold in half to form a loop. With matching sewing thread stitch raw edges of ribbon loop securely to WS of top of front heart. With RS facing, backstitch around front and back, leaving a small opening in one side. Turn to RS through opening, stuff lightly and close opening. Sew large white button to top centre front of heart.

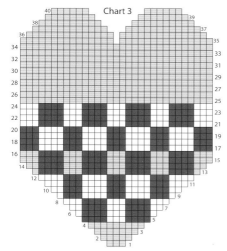

Chart 3

scented lavender bags

These delicate bags, decorated with

simple stitch-textured hearts, are trimmed

with a lacy edging and tied up with

pretty ribbons threaded through eyelets.

They are the perfect hand-knitted gift

and they don't take too long to make.

The lace edging and ribbon trim give these bags a vintage feel.

DESIGN SECRETS UNRAVELLED...

Lavender is of course the traditional filling for a scented sachet, but there's nothing to stop you using any dried herb of your choice. Why not knit your bag in the same colour as the dried flower or herb you are using? You could also use the bags to wrap any small gift – that way the lucky recipient gets two gifts in one!

YARN FOCUS

Use a fine weight (4ply) pure cotton yarn that has a slight sheen. This will show up stitch textures well and is available in a wide range of pastel and deep shades.

scented lavender bags

MEASUREMENTS

4in (10cm) wide and 5in (13cm) long,
including edging

GATHER TOGETHER...
materials

1 × 3½oz (100g) ball of fine weight (4ply) 100%
cotton yarn (361yd/330m per ball) in either:
A pale green for bag with reverse st st heart, or
B lilac for bag with st st heart

needles and notions

1 pair of size 2 (3mm) knitting needles
1yd (1m) of ³/₁₆in (5mm) wide satin ribbon

GAUGE (TENSION)

30 sts and 40 rows measure 4in (10cm) square
over st st on size 2 (3mm) needles

These small projects use simple stitches, but they also give you the chance to practise knitting lace and working a pattern from a chart.

knit your bag...
bag with reverse st st heart (pale green)
front

With size 2 (3mm) needles cast on 4 sts. K 1 row.
Work zigzag edging as foll:
1st row Sl 1, k1, (yo) 4 times, k2.
2nd row Sl 1, k1, (k1, p1, k1, p1) into next 4
strands on left needle, k2. 8 sts.
3rd–5th rows Sl 1, k to end.
6th row Bind (cast) off 4 sts, k to end.
Rep these 6 rows until 8 points in all have been
worked, ending with 5th row of final rep.
Next row Bind (cast) off all sts, keeping final st on
needle, pick up and k another 32 sts (4 sts from
each point) along straight edge. 33 sts.
Beg with a p row, work 9 rows in st st, ending with
a p row.
Work heart motifs in patt from chart, reading odd-
numbered (RS) rows from right to left and even-
numbered (WS) rows from left to right. When 20
rows of chart have been completed, work 12 more
rows in st st, ending with a p row.
**Next row (eyelet row) K4, yo, k2tog, *k6, yo, k2tog,
rep from * to last 3 sts, k3.
Next row P to end.
Next row K1, *p1, k1, rep from * to end.
Rep last row 3 times more to form seed (moss) st.

Bind (cast) off, working picot point edging as foll:
Next row Bind (cast) off 2 sts, *sl st from right to
left needle, cast on 2 sts, then bind (cast) off 4 sts,
rep from * to end. Fasten off, leaving a long end of
yarn for sewing up.

back

Make a slip knot on right needle, then pick up and
k33 sts along straight edge of zigzag edging on
opposite side. Beg with a p row, cont in st st until
back is level with eyelet row on front, ending with a
p row. Complete as given for front from ** to end.

bag with st st heart (lilac)

Work as given for Bag with Reverse St St Heart, but
work main fabric in reverse st st and hearts in st st.

to finish...

Press lightly according to directions on ball band.
Use long end of yarn to join side seams. Cut two
12in (30cm) lengths of ribbon. Starting and ending
at one side seam, thread one length of ribbon
through eyelets. Knot ends together and trim.
Repeat for the other ribbon, threading it from the
opposite side seam. Insert a lavender-filled sachet
and draw ribbons closed.

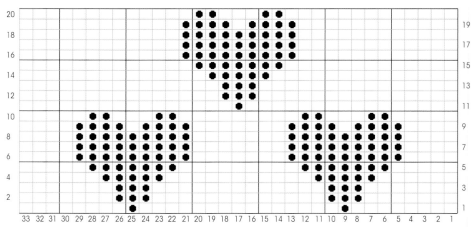

green shopping bag

Worked in an openwork mesh pattern, the top edge of this bag has an eye-catching display of yummy knitted vegetables. It's ideal for when you next hit the local market to stock up on the real thing – and it will provoke some delicious comments wherever you take it!

This bag is not only practical – it's fun, both to knit and to use!

DESIGN SECRETS UNRAVELLED...

If these veg aren't your favourites, why not use the patterns given as a template to invent your own versions? And if you prefer fruit, the patterns for the tomatoes and onion could easily become apples and oranges.

YARN FOCUS

The yarn used is a combination of 60% silk, 20% rayon and 20% cotton in a chunky weight. The silk content gives the yarn a subtle sheen, while the rayon and cotton provide strength. There is a good colour range with plenty of bright contemporary shades as well as some neutral ones.

green shopping bag

MEASUREMENTS

Bag measures approximately 13½in (35cm) wide and 15⅝in (40cm) long

GATHER TOGETHER...
materials

Bag: 5 × 1½oz (50g) balls of medium weight (aran) silk/rayon/cotton mix yarn (96yd/88m per ball)

Vegetables: Oddments of lightweight (DK) yarn in red, orange, pale yellow, white and green

needles and notions

1 pair of size 6 (4mm) knitting needles (veg only)
1 pair of size 7 (4.5mm) knitting needles
1 pair of size 8 (5mm) knitting needles
Stitch holders and markers
Small amount of polyester filling for vegetables
Large-eyed needle

GAUGE (TENSION)

18 sts and 24 rows measure 4in (10cm) square over garter stitch on size 8 (5mm) needles

The bag is worked in an easy mesh stitch, but you will need to take more care over the shaping and construction of the vegetables.

knit your bag...
bag back

With size 8 (5mm) needles cast on 51 sts.
Work base as foll: K 4 rows, inc 1 st at each end of 2nd and 4th rows. 55 sts. Place a marker at beg of next row to denote RS. Now work bag as foll:
Patt row K1, (yfwd, k2tog) 6 times, k8, (yfwd, k2tog) 7 times, k8, (yfwd, k2tog) 6 times.
Rep this row until work measures 13¾in (35cm) from beg, ending with a WS row.
Change to size 7 (4.5mm) needles.
Next row: K11, (yfwd, k2tog, k8, yfwd, k2tog, k10) twice.
Rep last row until work measures 15⅝in (40cm) from beg, ending with a WS row.

shape handles

Next row Bind (cast) off 10 sts, (k12 including st used to cast off, cast off 10 sts) twice. Fasten off.
Sl 12 sts from first handle onto a stitch holder. With WS facing, rejoin yarn to 12 sts for second handle.
Next row K2tog, k8, k2tog. 10 sts.

Next row (RS) K to end, working into the back of every st.
Next row K to end.
Rep last 2 rows until handle measures about 15⅝in (40cm), ending with a WS row. Cut off yarn and leave sts on a holder.
Place sts for first handle back onto a size 7 (4.5mm) needle. With WS facing, rejoin yarn and work to match first handle, ending with a RS row. Bind (cast) off sts from both handles tog, or graft them tog.

bag front

Work as given for back.

to finish...

Join side seams of bag to two rows above g st base. Join cast-on edges of base, then with seam placed flat along centre of base, join shaped sides of base to first two rows of bag to form corners. Make the vegetables and sew securely in place to front of bag, using the picture as a guide.

The addition of knitted vegetables makes this bag a truly unique piece.

vegetables

tomato (make 2)

With size 6 (4mm) needles and red DK yarn, cast on 6 sts.

1st row Kfb into each st to end. 12 sts.

2nd row P to end.

3rd row As 1st. 24 sts.

4th row (K1, p6) twice, (k1, p4) twice.

5th row (K1, m1, k2, m1, k1, p1) twice, (k1, m1, k4, m1, k1, p1) twice.

6th row (K1, p8) twice, (k1, p6) twice.

7th row (K1, m1, k4, m1, k1, p1) twice, (k1, m1, k6, m1, k1, p1) twice.

8th row (K1, p10) twice, (k1, p8) twice.

9th row (K8, p1) twice, (k10, p1) twice.

10th–16th rows Rep 8th and 9th rows 3 times, then work 8th row again.

17th row (K1, k2tog, k2, k2tog tbl, k1, p1) twice, (k1, k2tog, k4, k2tog tbl, k1, p1) twice. 32 sts.

18th row (K1, p1, p2tog tbl, p2, p2tog, p1) twice, (k1, p1, p2tog tbl, p2tog, p1) twice. 24 sts.

19th row (K2tog, k2tog tbl, p1) twice, (k1, k2tog, k2tog tbl, k1, p1) twice. 16 sts.

20th row (K1, p2tog tbl, p2tog) twice, (k1, p2tog tbl) twice. 10 sts.

21st row (K1, p1) twice, (k2tog, p1) twice. 8 sts.
Cut off yarn, leaving a long end and thread through rem sts.

to finish...

Place a small ball of polyester filling inside tomato. With RS facing and using thread from top of tomato, join seam, adding more filling if necessary. Thread a length of green yarn into a large-eyed needle and tie a large knot about 4in (10cm) up from one end. Insert through bottom of tomato. Push needle through to top centre of tomato and pull thread up slightly to give a tomato shape. Work a small stitch to secure. Now work 4 lazy daisy stitches in a cross shape on top of tomato. Fasten off end. Use long end at bottom of tomato to sew in place to front of bag.

onion

With size 6 (4mm) needles and pale yellow DK yarn, cast on 6 sts. Working in g st stripes of 2 rows each pale yellow and white, work as foll:

1st row Kfb into each st to end. 12 sts.

2nd row K to end.

3rd–4th rows As 1st and 2nd rows. 24 sts.

5th row (K1, m1, k2, m1, k3, m1, k4, m1, k2) twice.

6th row K to end.

7th row (K1, m1, k4, m1, k3, m1, k6, m1, k2) twice. Keeping stripe patt correct, work 13 rows straight.

21st row (K1, k2tog, k2, k2tog, k3, k2tog, k4, k2tog, k2) twice. 32 sts.

22nd row (K2, k2tog, k2, k2tog, k3, [k2tog] twice, k1) twice. 24 sts.

23rd row ([K2tog] twice, k2) 4 times. 16 sts.

24th row (K1, [k2tog] twice) twice, (k1, k2tog) twice. 10 sts.

25th row K1, (k2tog, k1) 3 times. 7 sts.

26th row K to end.
Join in green yarn and beg with a p row, work 9 rows in st st. Bind (cast) off.

to finish...

With WS of g st as RS, make a small ball of polyester filling and place inside the onion. Join seam, adding more stuffing if necessary.

carrot (make 3)

With size 6 (4mm) needles and orange DK yarn, cast on 6 sts.

1st row Kfb in each st to end. 12 sts.

2nd row K to end.

3rd row (Kfb, k2, kfb) 3 times. 18 sts.
Beg with a p row, work 16 rows in st st.

20th row P1, p2tog, p7, p2tog, p6. 16 sts.
Work 2 rows in st st.

23rd row (K6, k2tog) twice. 14 sts.
Work 3 rows in st st.

27th row K1, k2tog, k5, k2tog, k4. 12 sts.
Work 2 rows in st st.

30th row (P4, p2tog) twice. 10 sts.
Work 3 rows in st st.

34th row P1, p2tog, p3, p2tog, p2. 8 sts.

35th row K to end.

36th row (P2tog) 4 times. 4 sts.

37th row (K2tog) twice. 2 sts.

38th row P2tog and fasten off, leaving a long end.

to finish...

Beg at lower end, and with RS facing, start to stitch seam, adding small amounts of polyester filling as you progress until carrot is full. Thread a large-eyed needle with a length of green yarn and make 5 loop stitches, varying lengths, around top of carrot.

pea pod (make 2)

With size 6 (4mm) needles and green DK yarn, cast on 4 sts. Beg with a k row, work 4 rows in st st.

5th row Kfb in each st to end. 8 sts.

6th row P to end.

7th row As 5th row. 16 sts.

8th row P to end.

9th row K8, m1, k8. 17 sts.

10th row P to end.

11th row K8, mb, k8.
Work 3 rows in st st.

Next row As 11th row.
Rep last 4 rows 3 times more, then work 3 rows in st st.

Next row K2, (k2tog, k2) 3 times, k3. 14 sts.

Next row P to end.

Next row (K2tog) 7 times. 7 sts.

Next row P1, (p2tog) 3 times. 4 sts.
Work 4 rows in st st. Bind (cast) off.

to finish...

With RS facing join seam. Place seam at back of pea pod behind the bobbles and stitch through all layers, at either side of each bobble so that sides of pod come slightly over bobbles.

textured table runner

Jazz up the dining table with this brightly striped cotton runner that's a sampler of different basic fabrics and textured patterns. It's sure to make your dinner party go with a zing.

This is the ideal piece to bring a little colour and texture into your home.

DESIGN SECRETS UNRAVELLED...

Extend this runner by adding further panels of coloured and textured stitches. Brighten up your dining room by using the exciting colours chosen here, or coordinate with your home furnishings for a chic look. You can also experiment by using different types of yarn to create the different panels. Remember that highly textured yarns such as slubs, mohairs and chenille will hide all the hard work you put into knitting the patterned sections, so smooth cotton or machine-washable wool yarns are ideal for this project.

YARN FOCUS

This project uses a 100% cotton yarn with a slight twist to the fibres that is perfect for textured patterns. There is a fabulous colour range so you can choose all your favourite bright shades.

textured table runner

MEASUREMENTS
Finished runner measures 10in (25.5cm) wide
and 32in (81cm) long

GATHER TOGETHER...
materials
Lightweight (DK) 100% cotton yarn (95yd/84m
per 1½oz (50g) ball):
A 2 balls in red
B 1 ball in pale pink
C 1 ball in denim blue
D 1 ball in lime
E 1 ball in burgundy

needles
1 pair of size 6 (4mm) knitting needles

GAUGE (TENSION)
18 sts and 27 rows measure 4in (10cm) square
over st st on size 6 (4mm) needles

This straight strip with colour blocks of basic stitches is the perfect exercise in knitting patterns, but care must be taken to keep the knitting neat for a truly elegant look.

knit your runner...

With size 6 (4mm) needles and A, cast on 46 sts using the thumb method.
Cut off A and join in B. K 1 row.
Next row (WS) *K1, p1, rep from * to end.
Next row *P1, k1, rep from * to end.
Rep last 2 rows to form seed (moss) st until 23 rows in all have been worked, ending with a WS row.
Cut off B and join in A. Work 18 rows in g st, ending with a WS row.
Cut off A and join in C. K 1 row. Cont in diagonal rib patt.
1st row (WS) K2, *p3, k3, rep from * to last 2 sts, p2.
2nd row K3, *p3, k3, rep from * to last st, p1.
3rd row *P3, k3, rep from * to last 4 sts, p3, k1.
4th row P2, *k3, p3, rep from * to last 2 sts, k2.
5th row P1, *k3, p3, rep from * to last 3 sts, k3.
6th row K1, *p3, k3, rep from * to last 3 sts, p3.
Rep these 6 rows to form diagonal rib patt until 20 rows in all have been completed, ending with a RS row.
Cut off C and join in D. P 1 row.
Work 24 rows in seed (moss) st, ending with a WS row.
Cut off D and join in E. Work 16 rows in g st, ending with a WS row.
Cut off E and join in A. K 1 row. Cont in woven patt.
1st row (WS) *K5, p3, rep from * to last 6 sts, k6.
2nd row P6, *k3, p5, rep from * to end.
3rd row As 1st.
4th row K to end.
5th row K1, *p3, k5, rep from * to last 5 sts, p3, k2.
6th row P2, *k3, p5, rep from * to last 4 sts, k3, p1.
7th row As 5th.
8th row K to end.
Rep these 8 rows to form woven patt until 31 rows in all have been completed, ending with a WS row.
Cut off A and join in E. Work 16 rows in g st, ending with a WS row.

Cut off E and join in D. K 1 row. Work 25 rows in seed (moss) st, ending with a WS row.
Cut off D and join in C. K 1 row. Work 21 rows in diagonal rib patt, ending with a WS row.
Cut off C and join in A. Work 18 rows in g st, ending with a WS row.
Cut off A and join in B. K 1 row. Work 23 rows in seed (moss) st, ending with a WS row.
Cut off B and join in A. K 1 row. Bind (cast) off knitwise.

to finish...
Weave in all ends of yarn.
Pin out to finished size and, if necessary, press lightly with a warm iron over a dry cloth, taking care not to flatten the stitches.

breakfast set

Brighten up the breakfast table or tray with this cheery combination of tea cosy, placemat and egg cosies knitted in simple garter stitch and classic blue and cream. Let your knitted breakfast set make a great start to the day.

What better way to start the day than with this cheerful and traditional breakfast set?

DESIGN SECRETS UNRAVELLED...

The simplicity of garter stitch allows you free reign to choose your own colour scheme for this set. If you need help waking up in the morning, try knitting it in zingy citrus colours. Take the plunge and try this set in three colours rather than two.

YARN FOCUS

The yarn used is a good-looking and practical mixture of 55% wool, 25% acrylic and 20% nylon. It can be machine-washed on a gentle cycle and there are plenty of colours to choose from so you can coordinate with your own crockery.

breakfast set

Using only garter stitch and simple decreasing techniques, you will be able to knit yourself a stunning breakfast set in no time at all.

MEASUREMENTS

Tea cosy: to fit an average-sized teapot, width all round about 17in (44cm) and height 6½in (16cm), excluding bobble

Placemat: 11in (28cm) wide and 15in (38cm) long

Egg cosies: width all round 6½in (17cm) and height 3⅛in (8cm), excluding bobble

GATHER TOGETHER...
materials

Lightweight (DK) wool/acrylic/nylon yarn (131yd/120m per 1½oz (50g) ball): **A** blue, **B** cream

Tea cosy: 1 ball in each of A and B

Placemat: 2 balls in A and 1 in B

Egg cosies: (for 2) 1 ball in each of A and B

For complete set: 4 balls in A and 2 balls in B

needles

Tea cosy: 1 pair of size 3 (3.25mm) and size 5 (3.75mm) knitting needles

Placemat and egg cosies: 1 pair of size 8 (5mm) knitting needles

GAUGE (TENSION)

Tea cosy: 38 sts and 38 rows measure 4in (10cm) square over patt on size 5 (3.75mm) needles

Placemat and egg cosies: 17 sts and 32 rows measure 4in (10cm) square over g st with 2 strands of yarn and size 8 (5mm) needles

knit your tea cosy...

(Make 2 pieces alike)

With size 3 (3.25mm) needles and A, cast on 88 sts.

K 4 rows.

Change to size 5 (3.75mm) needles. Join in B and cont in patt, pulling yarn not in use quite tightly across WS of work to form pleats as foll:

1st row (RS) K2 B, (6 A, 6 B) to last 2 sts, 2 A.

2nd row Keeping yarn not in use at back of work, k2 A, (6 B, 6 A) to last 2 sts, 2 B.

Rep these 2 rows to form patt. Patt 44 more rows, ending with a WS row.

shape top

1st row K2 B, (6 A, 2 B, k2tog B, 2 B) to last 2 sts, 2 A. 81 sts.

2nd row K2 A, (5 B, 6 A) to last 2 sts, 2 B.

3rd row K2 B, (2 A, k2tog A, 2 A, 5 B) to last 2 sts, 2 A. 74 sts.

4th row K2 A, (5 B, 5 A) to last 2 sts, 2 B.

5th row K2 B, (5 A, 1 B, sl 1, k2tog, psso, 1 B) to last 2 sts, 2 A. 60 sts.

6th row K2 A, (3 B, 5 A) to last 2 sts, 2 B.

7th row K2 B, (1 A, sl 1, k2tog, psso, 1 A, 3 B) to last 2 sts, 2 A. 46 sts.

8th row K2 A, (3 B, 3 A) to last 2 sts, 2 B.

9th row K2 B, (keeping colours as set sl 1, k2tog, psso) to last 2 sts, 2 A. 18 sts.

Cut off yarn, thread through rem sts, draw up and fasten off securely.

to finish...

Join side seams, leaving openings for handle and spout. With B, make a pompom about 1½in (4cm) in diameter and sew securely to top of tea cosy.

1st row (RS) K2 A, (make bobble as foll – called MB): join in B, (k1, yfwd, k1, yfwd, k1) all in next st, turn and k5, turn and p2tog, p3tog, then pass 2nd st on right needle over 1st st, leaving 1 st in B on right needle, 9 A) twice, MB, 7 A.

2nd row With A, k7, (p1, k9) twice, p1, k2.

3rd–6th rows With A, k to end.

7th row K7 A, (MB, 9 A) twice, MB, 2 A.

8th row With A, k2, (p1, k9) twice, p1, k7.

9th–12th rows With A, k to end.

13th and 14th rows As 1st and 2nd.

With A, k 2 more rows. Complete as given for Striped Egg Cosy from * to end.

knit your placemat...

(Use yarn double throughout)

With size 8 (5mm) needles and A, cast on 45 sts. Cont in g st throughout, work (6 rows A and 6 rows B) twice, 74 rows A, (6 rows B and 6 rows A) twice. Bind (cast) off with A, but do not cut off yarn.

edging

With attached yarn A and RS of work facing, pick up and k 62 sts evenly down one long edge of mat (picking up 1 st for every 2 row ends). K 1 row. Bind (cast) off.

Work edging in same way along other long edge.

to finish...

Sew in ends and neaten corners.

knit your striped egg cosy...

(Use yarn double throughout)

With size 8 (5mm) needles and B, cast on 30 sts. Cont in g st throughout, work 3 rows B, 4 rows A, 4 rows B and 8 rows A.

shape top

*Cont in A only.

Next row (RS) K2, (k2tog, k4) to last 4 sts, k2tog, k2. 25 sts.

Next row K2, (k2tog, k3) to last 3 sts, k2tog, k1. 20 sts.

Next row K1, (k2tog, k2) to last 3 sts, k2tog, k1. 15 sts.

Next row (K1, k2tog) to end. 10 sts.

Next row (K2tog) to end. 5 sts.

Cut off yarn, thread through rem sts, draw up and fasten off securely.

to finish...

Fold egg cosy in half and join seam. With B, make a pompom about 1⅛ in (3cm) in diameter and stitch to top of cosy.

knit your spotted egg cosy...

(Use yarn double throughout)

With size 8 (5mm) needles and A, cast on 30 sts. Cont in g st throughout, work 3 rows. Cont in patt as foll:

flower power

A study in stockinette (stocking) stitch and colourful intarsia, this pillow/cushion has a stylized flower motif in each quarter and a buttoned centre back opening. It will look great in a contemporary setting.

This would be great as a gift for anyone with a contemporary approach to home décor.

DESIGN SECRETS UNRAVELLED...

This design lends itself to colour experimentation! There are so many combinations possible – knit several in contrasting colours for a bright and cheerful look. Consider working the flower patterns in a textured stitch to give a totally different look.

YARN FOCUS

The yarn used in this project is 100% merino wool. It is a luxuriously smooth yarn that gives good stitch definition and there are beautiful subtle and more colourful shades to choose from.

daisy pillow

MEASUREMENTS

18in (46cm) square

GATHER TOGETHER...

materials

2 x 1½oz (50g) balls of lightweight (DK) extra fine merino wool (127yd/116m per ball) in each of the following colours:

A red
B dark lilac
C light blue
D light sage green

needles and notions

1 pair of size 6 (4mm) knitting needles
4 buttons
18in (46cm) square cushion pad

GAUGE (TENSION)

22 sts and 28 rows measure 4in (10cm) square over st st on size 6 (4mm) needles

---

Four colours are interchanged, almost like an art print, to create this clever cushion. Working colour pattern from a chart requires skill for a neat finish (see page 113).

knit your pillow/cushion...

front

With size 6 (4mm) needles and B, cast on 51 sts, then on to same needle cast on another 51 sts with A. 102 sts. Twisting yarns tog on WS of work when changing colour to avoid a hole forming, cont as foll:

1st row (RS) K51 A, 51 B.
2nd row P51 B, 51 A.

Rep last 2 rows twice more. Now cont in patt from chart as foll:

1st row K4 A, k across 94 sts of 1st row of chart reading from right to left, k4 B.
2nd row P4 B, p across 94 sts of 2nd row of chart reading from left to right, p4 A. Cont in st st and patt from chart as set until 116 rows have been completed.

Next row K51 D, 51 C.
Next row P51 C, 51 D.

Rep last 2 rows twice more. Bind (cast) off in colour patt.

back

first piece (lower half)

With size 6 (4mm) needles and B, cast on 51 sts, then on to same needle cast on another 51 sts with A. 102 sts.

Twisting yarns tog on WS of work when changing colour to avoid a hole forming, cont as foll:

1st row (RS) K51 A, 51 B.
2nd row P51 B, 51 A.

Rep last 2 rows to form st st until piece measures 8⅝in (22cm) from beg, ending with a p row.

button band

Cont in colours as set, work in seed (moss) st as foll:

Next row (K1, p1) to end.
Next row (P1, k1) to end.

Rep last 2 rows 3 times more. Bind (cast) off in seed (moss) st.

second piece (top half)

With size 6 (4mm) needles and C, cast on 51 sts, then on to same needle cast on another 51 sts with D. 102 sts.

Twisting yarns tog on WS of work when changing colour to avoid a hole forming, cont as foll:

1st row (RS) K51 D, 51 C.
2nd row P51 C, 51 D.

Rep last 2 rows to form st st until piece measures 8⅝in (22cm) from beg, ending with a p row.

buttonhole band

Cont in colours as set, work in seed (moss) st as foll:

Next row (K1, p1) to end.
Next row (P1, k1) to end.
Next row (K1, p1) to end.
Next row Seed (moss) st 11, (yo, k2tog, seed (moss) st 24) 3 times, yo, k2tog, seed (moss) st 11. Work 4 more rows in seed (moss) st. Bind (cast) off in seed (moss) st.

to finish...

Carefully sew in all ends. Place front WS down and position backs on top, with RS facing and overlapping button band over buttonhole band in centre. Sew tog all round outer edge. Turn cushion cover RS out. Sew on buttons. Insert cushion pad and button closed.

daisy throw

MEASUREMENTS

57in (145cm) wide and 59in (150cm) long

GATHER TOGETHER...
materials

Super-bulky (super-chunky) 100% pure wool
(54yd/50m per 1½oz (50g) ball):

A 28 balls in sea green
B 5 balls in bright pink
C 1 ball in cream

needles and notions

1 pair of size 15 (10mm) knitting needles
1 pair of size 13 (9mm) double-pointed needles
or circular needle
Row counter

GAUGE (TENSION)

10 sts and 14 rows measure 4in (10cm) square
over st st on size 15 (10mm) needles

YARN FOCUS

The loose construction of the super-bulky
(super-chunky) yarn chosen for this throw
makes a soft fabric that is ideal for blankets
and throws, with plenty of shades to choose
from for exciting colour combinations.

This striking 'cheats' patchwork throw is worked in three long strips with chunky yarn and highlighted with appliquéd three-dimensional daisy flowers.

knit your throw...
left panel

With size 15 (10mm) needles and A, cast on
51 sts.
*P 4 rows.
Next row (RS) K to end.
Next row K2, p to last 2 sts, k2.
Rep last 2 rows 30 times more.
Work ridge as foll:
** **Next row** (RS) K2, p to last 2 sts, k2.
Rep last row 3 times more. **
Next row (RS) K to end.
Next row K2, p to last 2 sts, k2.
Rep last 2 rows 32 times more, then work as given
for ridge from ** to **.
Next row (RS) K to end.
Next row K2, p to last 2 sts, k2.
Rep last 2 rows 30 times more, then work as given
for ridge from ** to **. Cast off purlwise.*

centre panel

With size 15 (10mm) needles and A, cast on 52
sts. Work as given for left panel from * to *.

right panel

Work as given for left panel.

flowers (make 5)
petal (make 5 sets of 5 = 25 in total)

With size 13 (9mm) double-pointed needles or
circular needle and B, cast on 4 sts. K 1 row.
Next row *** Without turning work and RS facing,
slide sts to other end of needle and, pulling yarn
from left-hand side of sts to right across back, k1
tbl, k3.***
Rep from *** to ***, remembering to pull yarn tightly
across back and always working a k row, until cord
measures 45cm. Bind (cast) off.

---

centre (make 5)

With size 15 (10mm) needles and C, cast on 3 sts.
Cont in garter st, k 1 row, then inc 1 st at each end
of next 3 rows. 9 sts.
K 5 rows straight.
Dec 1 st at each end of next 3 rows. 3 sts. Bind
(cast) off.

to finish...

Sew the three panels together, using a one-stitch
seam on each edge. Bend each of five cords
needed for each flower into petal shape and pin
to the required square (using the photograph as
a guide) so that the ends of cord don't quite meet
in centre of the flower. Sew in place, then stitch
centres to middle of each flower to cover and
neaten ends of cords.

tea-time treats

Treat yourself to a traditional British afternoon tea with cakes that won't spoil your waistline. These decorative goodies are worked in fine weight (4ply) yarn and would make a great gift for a sweet-toothed friend. You can have fun knitting these delicious-looking treats again and again – you only have to count the stitches, not the calories!

This is an excellent project to practise using fine yarn and delicate finishing techniques.

YARN FOCUS

The yarn used is a practical mixture of 55% wool, 25% acrylic and 20% nylon. The wool-rich content of the yarn produces a good-looking fabric and there are plenty of fabulous colours to choose from.

tea-time treats

MEASUREMENTS

Battenberg cake: 2³/₈in (6cm) wide and 2½in (5.5cm) high

Chocolate cake: 2½in (7cm) wide, 4in (10cm) long and 2in (5cm) high

Cupcake: 2½in (7cm) in diameter and 3⅛in (8cm) high

Fondant fancies: 1½in (4cm) wide, 1⅝in (4.5cm) long and 1in (2.5cm) high

Doughnut: 3in (7.5cm) in diameter

GATHER TOGETHER...

materials

1 ×1½oz (50g) ball of fine weight (4ply) wool/acrylic/nylon mix yarn (201yd/184m per ball) in each of the following colours:

A pink
B lemon
C cream
D chocolate brown
E bronze
F cherry red
G white
H blue
I light green

1 ×3½oz (100g) ball of fine weight (4ply) 100% acrylic Courtelle yarn (410yd/375m per ball) in each of the following colours:

J lemon
K white

needles and notions

1 pair of size 2 (3mm) knitting needles

Set of four short size 2 (3mm) double-pointed needles (cupcake and doughnut only)

Polyester toy filling

Cardboard disc, 1³/₈in (3.5cm) in diameter (cupcake only)

Oddment of dark pink yarn (Battenberg cake only)

Selection of 2mm bugle beads in pink, yellow and blue (doughnut only)

Sewing needle and thread (for beads only)

GAUGE (TENSION)

28 sts and 36 rows measure 4in (10cm) square over st st on size 2 (3mm) needles

---

Because these cakes are constructed from a number of small pieces, they require a lot of attention to detail for a good finish and appearance.

knit your battenberg cake...

square ends of cake

With size 2 (3mm) needles, cast on 8 sts in A and 8 sts in B. 16 sts. Beg with a p row, work 10 rows in reverse st st, twisting yarns tog on WS of work when changing colour to avoid holes forming. Cut off yarn.

Next row (RS) K8 B, 8 A.

Beg with a k row, work 9 more rows in reverse st st with colours as set. Bind (cast) off with colours as set.

Work a second piece to match, but swapping colours on cast-on row and halfway through piece as before.

edging

With size 2 (3mm) needles and C, cast on 5 sts. Work 80 rows in st st. Bind (cast) off.

to finish...

Press according to directions. Join ends of edging strip tog. With RS facing, pin, then stitch edging around one square end. Repeat for other square end, leaving a gap in seam for turning through. Turn through and insert stuffing, then slipstitch seam closed. Work backstitch over colour change lines on square ends with darker pink yarn.

knit your chocolate cake...

top, end and bottom

With size 2 (3mm) needles and E, cast on 2 sts.
1st row K and inc in both sts. 4 sts.
Beg with a p row, cont in st st, inc 1 st at each end
of every foll 4th row until there are 20 sts. Work 2
more rows in st st, ending with a k row.
Next row K to end to mark foldline.
Beg with a k row, work 19 more rows st st.
Next row K to end to mark foldline.
Beg with a k row, work 2 more rows in st st. Cut off
E and join in D.
Work 2 rows in st st.
Next row (RS) Sl 1, k1, psso, k to last 2 sts, k2tog.
Cont to dec in this way on every foll 4th row until
2 sts rem.
Next row Sl 1, k1, psso and fasten off.

sides

With size 2 (3mm) needles, cast on 2 sts in E, 48
sts in D, 2 sts in E. 52 sts.

1st row (RS) K2 E, p48 D, k2 E.
2nd row P2 E, k48 D, p2 E.
Rep these 2 rows twice more.
Next row K2 E, 48 D, 2 E.
Next row P2 E, 48 F, 2 E.
Next row K to end in E.
Next row P2 E, 48 D, 2 E.
Work 1st and 2nd rows twice more, then work 1st
row again. Cut off D.

topping

Cont in E only, p 1 row and k 1 row. Bind (cast) off.

big cream swirls (make 2)

With size 2 (3mm) needles and C, cast on 20 sts.
1st row K, inc in each st. 40 sts.
P 1 row and k 1 row. Bind (cast) off.

small cream swirl

As big cream swirl, but cast on 8 sts and inc to
16 sts.

cherries (make 3)

With size 2 (3mm) needles and F, make a slip loop
on needle.
1st row (K1, p1) twice and k1 all into slip loop.
5 sts.
2nd row K, inc in each st. 10 sts.
P 1 row, k 1 row and p 1 row.
Next row (K2tog) 5 times, then pass 2nd, 3rd, 4th
and 5th sts over first st and off needle and fasten off.

to finish...

Press according to directions. Find and mark centre
of side sections on cast-on and bound-off (cast-off)
edges. With point of cast-on edge of top to marker
on bound-off (cast-off) edge of side section, so
matching parts in E, join seam, placing final marker
at point of bottom section and leaving a small gap.
Insert stuffing and close gap. Sew on cherries after
stuffing slightly. Twist cream swirls and sew on.

knit your fondant fancies...

base and 1st side

With size 2 (3mm) and K, cast on 10 sts. Beg with a k row, work 13 rows in st st. Cut off K and join in A or J. Work 9 more rows in st st, ending with a p row. Cut off yarn.

Next row With A or J, cast on 7 sts, k across 10 sts already on needle, turn and cast on 7 sts. 24 sts.

top, 2nd and 3rd sides

1st row P to end.
2nd row K to end.
3rd row P11, (m1, p1) twice, m1, p11.
4th row K to end.
5th row P16, turn and k5, turn and p to end.
6th row K to end.
7th and 8th rows As 5th and 6th rows.
9th row P11, (p2tog) 3 times, p10.
10th row K to end.
11th row P to end.
12th row Bind (cast) off 7 sts, k10, cast off 7 sts.

4th side

Beg with a p row, work 9 rows in st st. Bind (cast) off.

case

With size 2 (3mm) needles and K, cast on 9 sts. Work 70 rows in g st. Bind (cast) off.

to finish...

Press st st sections according to directions. Join row ends of sides to cast-on or bound-off (cast-off) edges of top, then sew two of the three edges around base (white square) to upper section. Stuff firmly and slipstitch open edge closed. Join cast-on and bound-off (cast-off) edges of case and stitch around sides of base. Backstitch lines in a contrast colour across top as shown in picture.

knit your cupcake...

With size 2 (3mm) double-pointed needles and G, cast on 15 sts evenly over 3 needles.

1st round (K1, m1) to end. 30 sts.

2nd and 3rd rounds K to end.

4th round *(K2, m1) 6 times, k3, m1, rep from * once more. 44 sts.

5th and 6th rounds K to end.

Cont in rounds of k1, p1 rib, work in stripes as foll: 3 rounds G, 1 round H, 7 rounds G, 1 round H and 3 rounds G. Cont in G, k 3 rounds.

Next round (picot) (Yfwd, k2tog) to end.

K 3 rounds, then k 4 rounds in E.

Next round (K9, k2tog) to end. 40 sts.

Cut off E and cont in G.

Next round (K8, k2tog) to end.

Next round (K7, k2tog) to end.

Cont to dec in this way on every round until 8 sts rem.

Next round (K2tog) 4 times.

Cut off yarn. Thread cut end through rem 4 sts, draw up and fasten off securely.

topping

Make 1 cherry as given for chocolate cake.

to finish...

Fold case at picot edge and sew through last row in K before change to E, working through both thicknesses to form edge of case. Insert filling through opening at base of case, then add cardboard disc to form flat bottom. Run a gathering thread through cast-on row, draw up and fasten off. Sew on cherry.

knit your doughnut...

With size 2 (3mm) double-pointed needles and E, cast on 30 sts evenly over 3 needles. K 6 rounds (to form st st).

Next round (K2, inc in next st) to end. 40 sts.

K 8 more rounds. Cut off E and join in I. K 11 rounds.

Next round (K2, k2tog) to end. 30 sts.

K 2 more rounds. Cut off I and join in E. K 4 rounds. Bind (cast) off.

to finish...

With RS of work facing, join bound-off (cast-off) round to cast-on round, leaving a small gap for filling. Insert filling and slipstitch opening closed. Sew on beads at random over 'iced' section, sewing on two at a time and more densely over top of doughnut.

paw-print
dog blanket

An irresistible doggy accessory, this patchwork-style blanket is worked in a combination of easy textures as well as a stylized intarsia paw-print motif. Who could resist this cosy blanket – certainly not Alfie, our canine model!

Add the finishing touch to this blanket with a border in double crochet.

DESIGN SECRETS UNRAVELLED...

Why not personalize your blanket even more by taking a paw print from your own pooch and using it as a basis to chart your own intarsia pattern? Create your chart on graph paper and substitute for the chart in the pattern. It is best to use graph paper designed especially for knitters – this is made up of rectangles rather than squares and will give you a better idea of how your finished design will look, since knitted stitches are also rectangles. Graph paper is freely available to download from many internet sites or check to see if your local yarn supplier carries it.

YARN FOCUS

This 100% Courtelle yarn makes the blanket soft and cosy for your pet, plus machine-washable as well. There is a wide range of colours to choose from so you can style your dog's bed to coordinate with your room scheme.

paw-print dog blanket

MEASUREMENTS
Approximately 20in (50cm) wide and
37in (95cm) long

GATHER TOGETHER...
materials
3 × 3½oz (100g) balls of bulky (chunky) 100%
Courtelle acrylic yarn (138yd/150m per ball)
in each of the following colours:
A black
B red

needles and notions
1 pair of size 9 (5.5mm) knitting needles
Size H-8 (5mm) crochet hook

GAUGE (TENSION)
13 sts and 20 rows measure 4in (10cm) square
over intarsia patt on size 9 (5.5mm) needles

Achieving the patchwork effect of this blanket is made easier by working in strips but working the intarsia pattern requires concentration.

knit your blanket...
(knitted in 5 strips)
1st strip
With size 9 (5.5mm) needles and A, cast on 25 sts.
Work 46 rows in g st.
Cut off A and join in B. Beg with a k row, cont in st st
and work 34 rows in patt from chart. Use B as main
colour (MC) and A as contrast colour (CC) and
read odd-numbered (k) rows from right to left and
even-numbered (p) rows from left to right. Cut off B.
Cont in A only, work 46 rows in g st. Bind (cast) off.

2nd strip
With size 9 (5.5mm) needles and B, cast on 25 sts.
Beg with a k row, cont in st st and work 34 rows in
patt from chart, using B as MC and A as CC. Cut
off B.
Cont in A only and work 46 rows in g st. Cut off A.
Cont in B only and chunky rib patt as foll:
1st row (RS) K to end.
2nd row K4, (p3, k4) to end.
Rep these 2 rows 19 times more. 40 rows in total.
Bind (cast) off.

3rd strip
With size 9 (5.5mm) needles and A, cast on 25 sts.
Work 46 rows in g st. Cut off A.
Cont in B only, work 40 rows in chunky rib patt as
given 2nd strip. Cut off B.
Join in A and beg with a k row, cont in st st and
work 34 rows in patt from chart, using A as MC and
B as CC. Bind (cast) off.

4th strip
With size 9 (5.5mm) needles and B, cast on 25 sts.
Work 40 rows in chunky rib patt as given for 2nd
strip. Cut off B.
Join in A and beg with a k row, cont in st st and
work 34 rows in patt from chart, using A as MC and
B as CC.
Cont in B only, work 46 rows in g st. Bind (cast) off.

5th strip
With size 9 (5.5mm) needles and A, cast on 25 sts.
Beg with a k row, cont in st st and work 34 rows in
patt from chart, using A as MC and B as CC.
Cont in B only, work 46 rows in g st. Cut off B.
Cont in A only, work 40 rows in chunky rib patt as
given for 2nd strip. Bind (cast) off.

to finish...
Join strips in order, from left to right, by oversewing
edges together on WS.

border
With H-8 (5mm) crochet hook, A and with RS of
work facing, join yarn to top edge of one strip, 1
chain, work in double crochet evenly around outer
edge of blanket, join with a slip stitch into first
chain. Cut off A. Using B, work another round of
double crochet into first round. Fasten off.

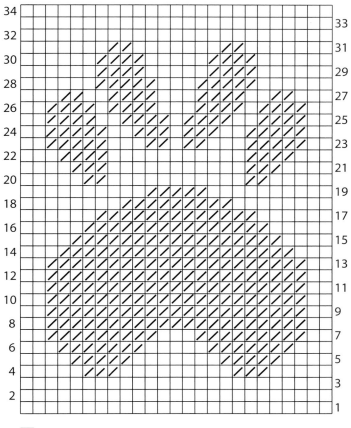

□ = MC

 = CC

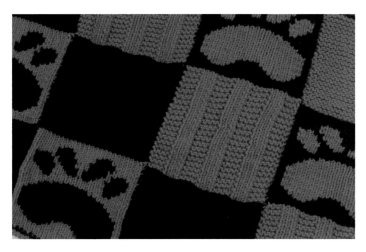

bathing beauties

After your bath, step on to your choice of cotton mats. The first is worked in stockinette (stocking) stitch with textured borders and eye-catching intarsia spots and matching fringes. The second is in garter stitch with stripes in contrasting cotton yarns. Why not splash out and knit both?

The fringe in a contrasting colour is the ideal embellishment for this attractive mat.

YARN FOCUS

This 100% pure cotton yarn is soft and absorbent – ideal for a bathmat. It comes in a wide range of shades for exciting colourwork.

DESIGN SECRETS UNRAVELLED...

Cotton is the ideal fibre for a bathmat, but that doesn't stop you experimenting with colour to coordinate with your bathroom. If you prefer, you could sew on a shop-bought tassel trim – but make sure that your trim has the same washing requirements as the yarn.

spotted bathmat

MEASUREMENTS
22in (55cm) wide and 32½in (83cm) long
(excluding tassels)

GATHER TOGETHER...
materials
100% pure cotton lightweight (DK) yarn
(95yd/84m per 1½oz (50g) ball):
A 12 balls in pale green
B 3 balls in teal

needles and notions
1 x pair of size 9 (5.5mm) knitting needles
Crochet hook for tassels

GAUGE (TENSION)
14 sts and 20 rows measure 4in (10cm) square
using yarn double on size 9 (5.5mm) needles

knit note: use 2 ends of A and B throughout.

This is a straightforward piece of knitting, but it takes concentration to place the spots correctly and keep the work neat.

knit your bathmat...
With size 9 (5.5mm) needles, A double and using thumb method, cast on 77 sts.
1st row (RS) K1, *p1, k1, rep from * to end.
Rep last row 5 times more to form seed (moss) st border.
Next row (RS) (K1, p1) twice, k69, (p1, k1) twice.
Next row (K1, p1) twice, p69, (p1, k1) twice.
Rep last 2 rows 8 times more. Cont in st st with seed (moss) st borders and working single spot patt as foll:
**Next row (RS) With A, (k1, p1) twice, k33 A, 4 B from 1st row of spot chart, 32 A, (p1, k1) twice.
Cont in patt as set until 10 rows of chart have been completed. When working from chart, read odd-numbered (RS) rows from right to left and even-numbered (WS) rows from left to right and twist yarns tog on WS of work when changing colours to avoid holes forming.
Work 8 more rows in A only, then work double spot patt as foll:
Next row (RS) With A, (k1, p1) twice, k11 A, 4 B from 1st row of spot chart, 40 A, 4 B from 1st row of spot chart, 10 A, (p1, k1) twice.
Cont in patt as set until 10 rows of chart have been completed. Work 8 more rows in A only. Rep from ** twice more, then work 10 rows with single spot patt as before.
Cut off B.
Work 18 rows in st st with seed (moss) st borders, ending on WS, then work 6 rows in seed (moss) st. Bind (cast) off purlwise.

to finish...
Darn in ends carefully. Press according to directions on ball band. Cut B into 7in (18cm) lengths. Taking 8 strands tog each time and using a crochet hook, knot fringes along each short end of mat (working one tassel at each end with 11 more evenly spaced between). Trim finished fringes to about 2½in (6.5cm) long.

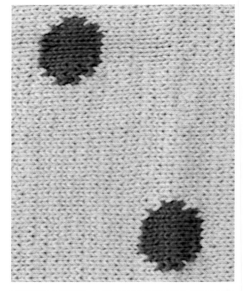

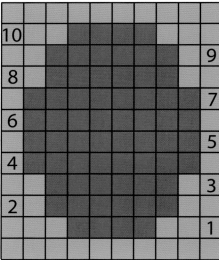

☐ = A

■ = B

striped bathmat

MEASUREMENTS
17in (44cm) wide and 27in (69cm) long

GATHER TOGETHER...
materials
1 6 × 1½oz (50g) balls of braid/ribbon yarn in a 68% cotton/22% viscose/10% linen mix (46yd/50m per ball) in blue

2 5 × 1½oz (50g) balls of bulky (chunky) 55% cotton/45% acrylic mix yarn (58yd/63m per ball) in turquoise

3 3 × 1½oz (50g) balls of bulky (chunky) 55% cotton/45% acrylic mix yarn (58yd/63m per ball) in white

4 2 × 1½oz (50g) balls of medium weight (aran) 60% cotton/40% acrylic/microfibre mix yarn (97½yd/90m per ball) in pale blue

needles
1 pair of size 17 (12.75mm) needles

GAUGE (TENSION)
7½ sts and 14 rows measure 4in (10cm) square over g st on size 17 (12.75mm) needles.

YARN FOCUS
An interesting assortment of yarns are used to create the texture: a braid yarn, rope-like cotton and a finer cotton are used together to create four strands and then a plain colour is used, again as four strands, to make the contrast stripes.

knit note: the rug is knitted using 4 strands of yarn held together throughout as follows:
***A** 2 strands of no. 1, 1 strand of no. 3 and 1 strand of no. 4*
***B** 4 strands of no. 2*

The rows of interlocking stitches look the same on both sides of the fabric, so your mat will be reversible.

knit your bathmat...
With size 17 (12.75mm) needles and A, cast on 33 sts. Work 6 rows in g st, ending with a WS row. Continue in g st throughout and work in stripe sequence as follows:
1st and 2nd rows Work in B.
3rd to 8th rows Work in A.
9th and 10th rows Work in B.
11th to 14th rows Work in A.
15th and 16th rows Work in B.
17th and 18th rows Work in A.
19th and 20th rows Work in B.
21st and 22nd rows Work in A.
23rd and 24th rows Work in B.
25th to 28th rows Work in A.
29th and 30th rows Work in B.
31st to 36th rows Work in A.
37th and 38th rows Work in B.
39th to 46th rows Work in A.
47th to 84th rows As 1st to 38th rows.
85th to 91st rows Work in A.
Bind (cast) off knitwise on WS of work.

to finish...
Press the completed mat with a warm iron over a damp cloth. When you complete the mat there will be ends of textured and plain-coloured yarn at the edges. These should be sewn into the fabric so they are invisible, but you will probably need to do this by splitting the yarn into several threads at a time as all of the threads will not pass through the eye of a wool needle.

storage pockets

Keep clutter at bay in a child's room with this rainbow-bright storage system of pockets, decorated with spots and stripes. Hang these brightly-coloured pockets on a door or wall and use them as a home for all those favourite bits and pieces.

There is plenty of room in the pockets to store lots and lots of treasure.

DESIGN SECRETS UNRAVELLED…
Although this design is very practical and made in easily cleanable yarn, it is also very decorative. You could also use it as a wall hanging and embellish it with buttons, sequins or other trims. Remember that if you do this, it will need careful, gentle cleaning rather than a quick swish round in the washing machine.

YARN FOCUS
This cotton yarn is ideal for this design as it is available in a variety of bright shades that will appeal to children. And when it gets dirty, it can be popped into the washing machine.

storage pockets

MEASUREMENTS
Finished storage pockets measure
20in (50cm) square

GATHER TOGETHER...
materials
Lightweight (DK) 100% pure cotton yarn
(95yd/84m per 1½oz (50g) ball) in the
following colours:
A 8 balls in indigo
B 1 ball in red
C 1 ball in orange
D 1 ball in yellow
E 1 ball in turquoise
F 1 ball in blue
G 1 ball in violet

needles and notions
1 pair of size 5 (3.75mm) knitting needles
4 buttons
Hanging pole

GAUGE (TENSION)
21 sts and 30 rows measure 4in (10cm) over st st
on size 5 (3.75mm) needles

Despite looking quite complex, all you need to use is straightforward stockinette (stocking) stitch fabric and a little shaping, together with some intarsia work.

knit your storage pockets...
With size 5 (3.75mm) needles and A, cast on 105 sts. Beg with a k row, work 4 rows in st st.
Next row P to end to mark hemline.
Beg with a p row, work 17 rows in st st.
*__Next row__ Inc in every st by working into front and back of each st.
Thread every alt st on to a piece of contrast-coloured waste yarn and secure.
Cont working on rem 105 sts. Beg with a p row, work 65 rows in st st. * Rep from * to * once more.
Next row P to end to mark hemline.
Beg with a p row, work 3 rows in st st. Bind (cast) off.

first row of pockets
With RS facing and working from left to right, sl sts from 1st row of 105 sts being held on to a size 5 (3.75mm) needle. Cont in st st and patt from chart. Join in and cut off colours as required. Use small separate balls of yarn for dots and twist yarns tog on WS of work when changing colour to avoid holes forming. Place patt as foll:
1st row (RS) K38 E for striped section, 19 A, 3 B, 7 A, then 38 E for striped section.
2nd row P38 E for striped section, 6 A, 5 B, 18 A, 38 E for striped section.
Cont in st st and patt from chart (referring to photograph for colour of dots and colour sequence chart for stripes) until 36 rows are complete.

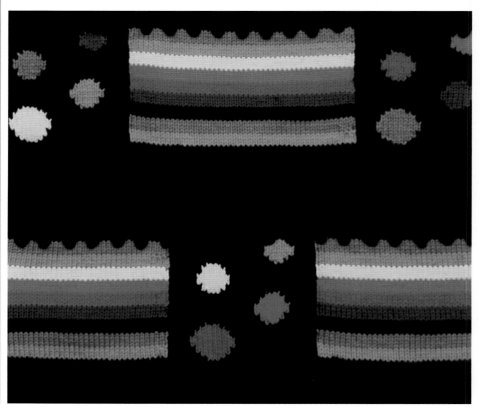

SPECIAL ABBREVIATION
mb (make bobble) (k1, p1, k1, p1) all into next st, turn and p4, turn and k4, turn and p4, turn and sl 1, k3tog, psso

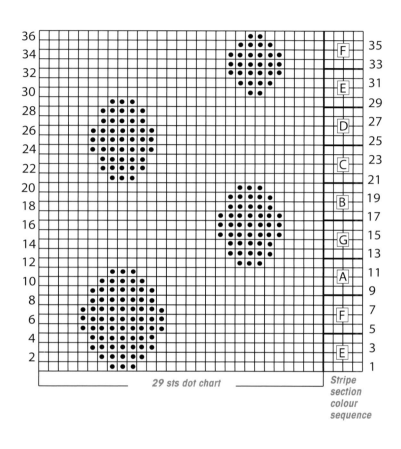

36
34
32
30
28
26
24
22
20
18
16
14
12
10
8
6
4
2

35
33
31
29
27
25
23
21
19
17
15
13
11
9
7
5
3
1

F
E
D
C
B
G
A
F
E

29 sts dot chart

Stripe section colour sequence

KEY

☐ = A

⊡ = contrast colour (see photo)

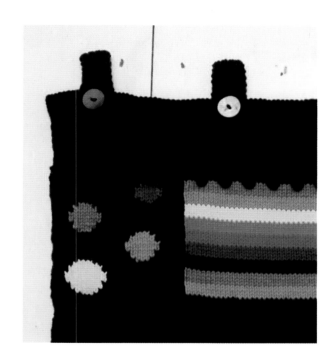

Cont in A only and work bobble trim.

1st row (RS) K to end.

2nd row P to end.

3rd row K2, *(mb), k4, rep from * to last 3 sts, mb, k2

4th row P to end.

Bind (cast) off.

second row of pockets

With RS facing and working from left to right, sl sts from 2nd row of 105 sts being held, on to a size 5 (3.75mm) needle. Place patt from chart as foll:

1st row (RS) K19 A, 3 F, 7 A, 47 E for striped section, 19 A, 3 D, 7 A.

2nd row P6 A, 5 D, 18 A, 47 E for striped section, 6 A, 5 F, 19 A.

Cont in st st and patt from chart (referring to photograph for colour of dots and colour sequence

for stripes) until 36 rows are completed.

Cont in A only, work 4 rows as given for bobble trim.

Bind (cast) off.

tab tops (make 4)

With size 5 (3.75mm) needles and A, cast on 9 sts.

1st rib row (P1, k1) to last st, p1.

2nd rib row (K1, p1) to last st, k1.

Rep these 2 rows 15 times more.

Buttonhole row (P1, k1) twice, yfwd, k2tog, p1, k1, p1.

Next row (K1, p1) to last st, k1.

shape point

1st row K2tog, (p1, k1) twice, p1, k2tog.

2nd row (P1, k1) to last st, k1.

3rd row P2tog, k1, p1, k1, p2tog.

4th row (K1, p1) to last st, k1.

5th row K2tog, p1, k2tog.

6th row P1, k1, p1.

7th row K3tog and fasten off.

to finish...

Carefully stitch in all ends on WS of work, taking particular care at edge. Steam and block the piece of work to size. Turn hems at top and bottom edge to WS at hemline and slipstitch in place. Sew vertical lines of backstitch up edges of pockets and at points where pattern changes to create 6 individual pockets. Sew straight edge of tabs firmly in place 1in (2.5cm) below top edge on RS, spacing one 2in (5cm) in from each side edge, with the remaining two evenly spaced between. Sew buttons in place on RS of hanging to correspond with buttonholes and button around a hanging pole.

perfectly patterned

A hand-knitted throw is a priceless treasure, especially this one as it is richly textured with cable patterns. Knitting it in three separate panels makes it easy to handle. Classic cable design and a soft chunky yarn make this a wonderful throw to keep you snug on chilly winter evenings.

The traditional cable patterns and luxurious yarn give this throw an air of timeless elegance.

DESIGN SECRETS UNRAVELLED...

Highly textured designs are best worked in smooth yarn to show off the intricacy of the stitches. Do not be tempted to substitute yarns with a texture or pile, such as bouclé or chenille, as the cable pattern will disappear and lose its impact.

YARN FOCUS

This yarn is a luxurious blend of 75% extra fine merino wool with 20% silk and 5% cashmere. It is available in incredibly soft beautiful subtle shades for making irresistible textured knits.

aran throw

MEASUREMENTS
49in (125cm) wide and 60in (154cm) long

GATHER TOGETHER...
materials
31 × 1½oz (50g) balls of medium weight (aran) extra fine merino wool/silk/cashmere mix yarn (94yd/86m per ball) in blue

needles and notions
1 pair of size 6 (4mm) knitting needles
1 pair of size 8 (5mm) knitting needles
Cable needle

GAUGE (TENSION)
18 sts and 24 rows to 4in (10cm) square over st st worked on size 8 (5mm) needles

SPECIAL ABBREVIATIONS
BC sl 1 st on to cn and leave at back of work, k2, then p1 from cn
FC sl 2 sts on to cn and leave at front of work, p1, then k2 from cn
C3B sl 1 st on to cn and leave at back of work, k2, then k1 from cn
C3F sl 2 sts on to cn and leave at front of work, k1, then k2 from cn
C4 sl 2 sts on to cn and leave at back of work, k2, then k2 from cn
C8B sl 4 sts on to cn and leave at back of work, k4, then k4 from cn
C8F sl 4 sts on to cn and leave at front of work, k4, then k4 from cn

The construction of the throw as a straight strip with no shaping leaves you free to concentrate on the various cable stitches.

knit your throw...
Note: throw is made up of three panels:
panel one – to the right of centre panel as you look at it
panel two – centre panel
panel three – to the left of centre panel as you look at it

pattern A
(worked over 12 sts)
1st row (WS) k1, p10, k1.
2nd row P4, C4, p4.
3rd row K4, p4, k4.
4th row P3, C3B, C3F, p3.
5th row K3, p6, k3.
6th row P2, C3B, k2, C3F, p2.
7th row K2, p8, k2.
8th row P1, C3B, k4, C3F, p1.
These 8 rows form patt and are repeated throughout.

pattern B
(worked over 20 sts)
1st row (WS) K3, p2, k3, p4, k3, p2, k3.
2nd row (P2, BC) twice, (FC, p2) twice.
3rd and every foll WS row K all k sts and p all p sts.
4th row P1, (BC, p2) twice, FC, p2, FC, p1.
6th row (BC, p2) twice, (p2, FC) twice.
8th row (FC, p2) twice, (p2, BC) twice.

10th row P1, (FC, p2) twice, BC, p2, BC, p1.
12th row (P2, FC) twice, (BC, p2) twice.
These 12 rows form patt and are repeated throughout.

panel one
With size 6 (4mm) needles cast on 75 sts. Work 10 rows in g st.
Inc row (RS) K23, *m1, k3, m1, k2, rep from * 6 times more, m1, k17. 90 sts.
Change to size 8 (5mm) needles. Cont in patt as foll:
1st row (WS) P18, k2, p2, (k2, p8, k2, p2) 3 times, k2, p18, k6.
2nd row K24, p2, k2, (p2, k8, p2, k2) 3 times, p2, k18.
3rd row As 1st row.
4th row As 2nd row.
5th row As 1st row.
6th row K24, p2, k2, (p2, C8B, p2, k2) 3 times, p2, k18.
7th row As 1st row.
8th row As 2nd row.
9th row As 1st row.
10th row As 2nd row.
11th row As 1st row.
12th row As 2nd row.
These 12 rows form patt and are repeated throughout. Rep them 29 times more.
Change to size 6 (4mm) needles.
Dec row (WS) K17, *k2tog, k2, k2tog, k1, rep from * 6 times more, k2tog, k22. 75 sts.
Work 9 rows in g st. Bind (cast) off fairly loosely.

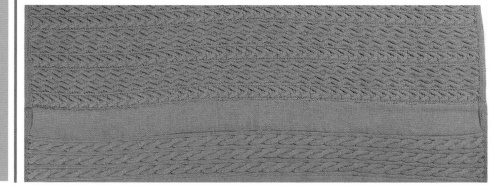

panel two

With size 6 (4mm) needles cast on 79 sts. Work 10 rows in g st.

Inc row (RS) K1, *m1, k2, rep from * 37 times more, m1, k2. 118 sts.

Change to size 8 (5mm) needles. Cont in patt as foll:

1st row (WS) K1, p1, *work 1st row from Patt A over next 12 sts, p1, work 1st row from Patt B over next 20 sts, p1, rep from * 3 times in all, work 1st row from Patt A over next 12 sts, p1, k1.

2nd row K1, k1b, *work 2nd row from Patt A over next 12 sts, k1b, work 2nd row from Patt B over next 20 sts, k1b, rep from * 3 times in all, work 2nd row from Patt A over next 12 sts, k1b, k1.

3rd row K1, p1, *work 3rd row from Patt A over next 12 sts, p1, work 3rd row from Patt B over next 20 sts, p1, rep from * 3 times in all, work 3rd row from Patt A over next 12 sts, p1, k1.

4th row K1, k1b, *work 4th row from Patt A over next 12 sts, k1b, work 4th row from Patt B over next 20 sts, k1b, rep from * 3 times in all, work 4th row from Patt A over next 12 sts, k1b, k1.

Cont in patt as set until Patt B has been worked 30 times in all.

Change to size 6 (4mm) needles.

Dec row (WS) K1, *k2tog, k1, rep from * to end. 79 sts.

Work 9 rows in g st. Bind (cast) off fairly loosely.

panel three

With size 6 (4mm) needles cast on 75 sts. Work 10 rows in g st.

Inc row (RS) K17, *m1, k3, m1, k2, rep from * 6 times more, m1, k23. 90 sts.

Change to size 8 (5mm) needles. Cont in patt as foll:

1st row (WS) K6, p18, k2, p2, (k2, p8, k2, p2) 3 times, k2, p18.

2nd row K18, p2, k2, (p2, k8, p2, k2) 3 times, p2, k24.

3rd row As 1st row.

4th row As 2nd row.

5th row As 1st row.

6th row K18, p2, k2, (p2, C8F, p2, k2) 3 times, p2, k24.

7th row As 1st row.

8th row As 2nd row.

9th row As 1st row.

10th row As 2nd row.

11th row As 1st row.

12th row As 2nd row.

These 12 rows form patt and are repeated throughout. Rep them 29 times more.

Change to size 6 (4mm) needles.

Dec row (WS) K22, *k2tog, k2, k2tog, k1, rep from * 6 times more, k2tog, k17. 75 sts.

Work 9 rows in g st. Bind (cast) off fairly loosely.

to finish...

Press lightly according to instructions on ball band. Sew panels together neatly. Press seams lightly.

textured laundry bag

MEASUREMENTS

Bag measures 13½in (35cm) across base and
22in (56cm) high

GATHER TOGETHER...
materials

12 × 1½oz (50g) balls of cotton/acrylic mix yarn
(100yd/92m per ball) in light blue

needles

1 pair of size 5 (3.75mm) knitting needles
1 pair of size 6 (4mm) knitting needles

GAUGE (TENSION)

20 sts and 26 rows measure 4in (10cm) square
over st st on size 6 (4mm) needles

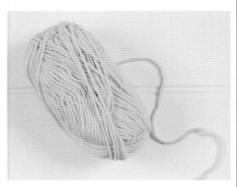

YARN FOCUS

This bag is made in a practical yarn with a 50%
cotton and 50% acrylic mixture. Slightly softer
than pure cotton yarn, it can be machine-washed
at a low temperature and the palette of 'washed'
colours is good to choose from.

This drawstring bag features textured diamonds – as an all-over pattern and as
motifs in the border. The main section consists of a straight piece in a simple
knit and purl stitch pattern, but there are a lot of stitches to cope with.

knit your bag...
base

With size 6 (4mm) needles cast on 12 sts. Beg
with a k row, cont in st st. Work 1 row. Cast on 4
sts at beg of next 4 rows, then 3 sts at beg of foll 2
rows. 34 sts.
Inc 1 st at each end of next 8 rows. 50 sts.
Work 1 row, ending with a WS row.
Inc 1 st at each end of next and 7 foll alt rows, then
on 2 foll 4th rows. 70 sts.
Work 15 rows, ending with a WS row.
Dec 1 st at each end of next and 2 foll 4th rows,
then on 7 foll alt rows. 50 sts.
Work 1 row, ending with a WS row. Dec 1 st at each
end of next 8 rows. 34 sts.
Bind (cast) off 3 sts at beg of next 2 rows, then 4
sts at beg of foll 4 rows, ending with a WS row. Bind
(cast) off rem 12 sts.

main section

With size 6 (4mm) needles cast on 217 sts. Work
in g st for 6 rows, ending with a WS row. Cont in
border patt:
1st row (RS) K to end.
2nd row P to end.
3rd and 4th rows As 1st and 2nd rows.
5th row K9, p1, *k17, p1, rep from * to last 9 sts, k9.
6th row P9, k1, *p17, k1, rep from * to last 9 sts, p9.
7th row K8, p1, k1, p1, *k15, p1, k1, p1, rep from *
to last 8 sts, k8.
8th row P8, k1, p1, k1, *p15, k1, p1, k1, rep from *
to last 8 sts, p8.
9th row K7, (p1, k1) twice, p1, *k13, (p1, k1) twice,
p1, rep from * to last 7 sts, k7.
10th row P7, (k1, p1) twice, k1, *p13, (k1, p1)
twice, k1, rep from * to last 7 sts, p7.
11th row K6, (p1, k1) 3 times, p1, *k11, (p1, k1) 3
times, p1, rep from * to last 6 sts, k6.
12th row P6, (k1, p1) 3 times, k1, *p11, (k1, p1) 3
times, k1, rep from * to last 6 sts, p6.
13th row K5, p1, k1, p1, k3, p1, k1, p1, *k9, p1, k1,

p1, k3, p1, k1, p1, rep from * to last 5 sts, k5.
14th row P5, k1, p1, k1, p3, k1, p1, k1, *p9, k1, p1,
k1, p3, k1, p1, k1, rep from * to last 5 sts, p5.
15th row K4, p1, k1, p1, k5, p1, k1, p1, *k7, p1, k1,
p1, k5, p1, k1, p1, rep from * to last 4 sts, k4.
16th row P4, k1, p1, k1, p5, k1, p1, k1, *p7, k1, p1,
k1, p5, k1, p1, k1, rep from * to last 4 sts, p4.
17th and 18th rows As 13th and 14th rows.
19th and 20th rows As 11th and 12th rows.
21st and 22nd rows As 9th and 10th rows.
23rd and 24th rows As 7th and 8th rows.
25th and 26th rows As 5th and 6th rows.
27th and 28th rows As 1st and 2nd rows.
29th–34th rows K to end.
These 34 rows complete border patt.
Next row (RS) K8, k2tog, *k16, k2tog, rep from * to
last 9 sts, k9. 205 sts.
Next row P1, k1, *p9, k1, p1, k1, rep from * to last
11 sts, p9, k1, p1.
Cont in diamond patt:
1st row (RS) P1, k1, p1, k7, *(p1, k1) twice, p1, k7,
rep from * to last 3 sts, p1, k1, p1.
2nd row (P1, k1) twice, p5, *(k1, p1) 3 times, k1,
p5, rep from * to last 4 sts, (k1, p1) twice.
3rd row K2, p1, k1, p1, *k3, p1, k1, p1, rep from * to
last 2 sts, k2.
4th row P3, (k1, p1) 3 times, k1, *p5, (k1, p1) 3
times, k1, rep from * to last 3 sts, p3.
5th row K4, (p1, k1) twice, p1, *k7, (p1, k1) twice,
p1, rep from * to last 4 sts, k4.
6th row P5, k1, p1, k1, *p9, k1, p1, k1, rep from * to
last 5 sts, p5.
7th row As 5th row.
8th row As 4th row.
9th row As 3rd row.
10th row As 2nd row.
11th row As 1st row.
12th row P1, k1, *p9, k1, p1, k1, rep from * to last
11 sts, p9, k1, p1.
These 12 rows form diamond patt. Cont in patt until
main section measures approximately 20in (51cm)

from cast-on edge, ending with 6th or 12th row of patt.

Change to size 5 (3.75mm) needles. Work top casing:

Next row (RS) K102, k2tog, k101. 204 sts.
Work in g st for 5 rows, ending with a WS row. Beg with a k row, work in st st for 2 rows.

divide for opening
Next row (RS) K102, turn and work this side first.
Next row K1, p to end.
Next row K to end.
Rep last 2 rows once more. Cut off yarn and leave these 102 sts on a spare needle.
With RS facing, rejoin yarn to rem 102 sts, k to end.
Next row P to last st, k1.
Next row K to end.
Rep last 2 rows once more.
Next row P102, then p102 sts from spare needle. 204 sts.
Next row K to end.
Next row K to end (to form g st ridge).
Beg with a k row, work in st st for 8 rows, ending with a WS row. Using size 6 (4mm) needle, bind (cast) off.

to finish...
Do not press.

Join row-end edges of main section. Fold top edge of main section to WS at ridge row, then sew bound-off (cast-off) edge in place. Sew main section to base.

Using 3 strands of yarn, make a twisted cord approximately 59in (150cm) long. Thread through casing.

Using 3 strands of yarn, make a twisted cord approximately 8in (20cm) long. Fold in half and sew to inside of casing at seam to form hanging loop.

it's all in
the detail...

casting on – thumb method

There are several different ways to cast on stitches and you probably have your own favourite method. However, some methods are better than others if you want to achieve certain results, so it is always best to use the method specified in the pattern – the designer will have chosen it for a reason. Here are instructions for the two methods used in the patterns in this book.

THUMB METHOD

This method uses only one needle and is the simplest way of casting on.

Unwind a length of yarn from the ball that is enough for the number of stitches you are casting on. Allow approximately 1–1⅛in (2.5–3cm) per stitch. Make a slip knot at this point on one needle.

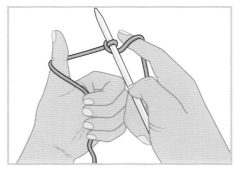

1 Hold the needle with the slip knot in your right hand. Put the ball end of the yarn over the index finger, under the middle finger and over the third finger of your right hand. Wrap the free end of the yarn around the thumb of your left hand from the back.

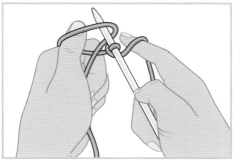

2 Insert the needle through the thumb loop from front to back.

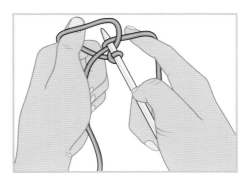

3 Using the index finger of your right hand, wrap the yarn from the ball around the needle.

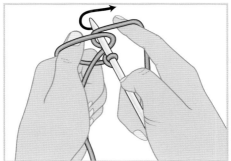

4 Pull the loop on the needle through the loop on your thumb. Slip the loop off your thumb and gently tighten the stitch up to the needle by pulling on both strands of yarn. Repeat until you have cast on the required number of stitches.

casting on – cable method

It is important not to cast on too tightly. If you do, your edge may not be sufficiently elastic and may break. If you tend to cast on too tightly, try using needles a size larger than required to knit the main fabric. Make sure you change back to the needle size given in the pattern before you start knitting your item.

CABLE METHOD

Cable cast-on gives a neat, firm edge that is also elastic because more yarn has been introduced into the casting-on process; this makes it perfect as an edging for rib stitch, which has to have elasticity. It is also the method used to cast on stitches in the middle of a row. This method uses two needles.

Make a slip knot about 6in (15cm) from the end of the yarn on one needle. Hold this needle in your left hand.

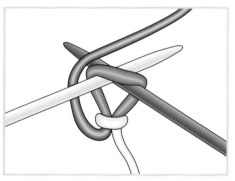

1 Insert the right-hand needle knitwise into the loop on the left-hand needle and wrap the yarn around the tip.

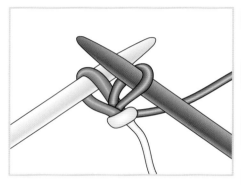

2 Pull the yarn through the loop to make a stitch but do not drop the stitch off the left-hand needle.

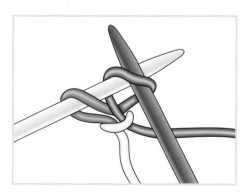

3 Slip the new stitch onto the left-hand needle by inserting the left-hand needle into the front of the loop from right to left. You will now have two stitches on the left-hand needle.

4 Insert the right-hand needle between the two stitches on the left-hand needle and wrap the yarn around the tip. Pull the yarn back through between the two stitches and place it on the left-hand needle, as shown in step 3.

Repeat step 4 until you have cast on the required number of stitches.

knit stitch

This is the simplest stitch of all and is the one that most people learn first. Once you have mastered the knit stitch, you can create a number of the projects featured in this book.

MAKING THE KNIT STITCH

Each stitch is created with a four-step process. Hold the yarn at the back of the work – this is the side facing away from you.

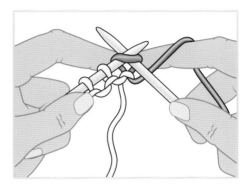

1 Place the needle with the cast-on stitches in your left hand, insert the right-hand needle into the front of the first stitch on the left-hand needle from left to right.

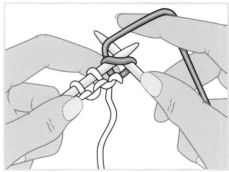

2 Take the yarn around and under the point of the right-hand needle.

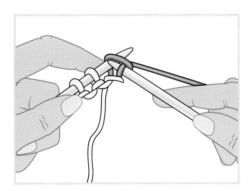

3 Draw the new loop on the right-hand needle through the stitch on the left-hand needle.

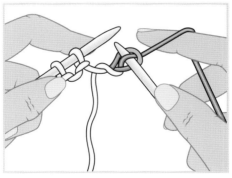

4 Slide the stitch off the left-hand needle. This has formed one knit stitch on the right-hand needle.

Repeat these four steps until all stitches on the left-hand needle have been transferred to the right-hand needle. This is the end of the row. Swap the right-hand needle into your left hand and begin the next row in exactly the same way.

GARTER STITCH

Rows of knit stitch build up to form an interlocking fabric, which is called garter stitch (g st). It has ridges on the front and back and is identical from either side, so it is reversible. It forms a flat and fairly thick fabric that does not curl at the edges.

purl stitch

This is the reverse of the knit stitch. Once you know purl stitch, you can make any of the patterns in this book.

STOCKINETTE (STOCKING) STITCH

This stitch is the basis of many knitwear items as it has a flat and tightly woven appearance. It is created by making alternate knit and purl rows. The knit rows are the right side of the fabric and the purl rows are the wrong side. Instructions for stockinette (stocking) stitch in knitting patterns can be written as follows:

Row 1 RS Knit
Row 2 Purl

Or alternatively:
Work in st st, beg with a k row.

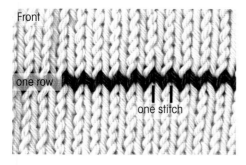

Front
one row
one stitch

REVERSE STOCKINETTE (STOCKING) STITCH

Reverse stockinette (stocking) stitch (rev st st) is when the back of stockinette (stocking) stitch is used as the right side of the fabric. So, the purl rows are the right side and the knit rows are the wrong side. It is often used as the background stitch in cable patterns and is effective when used as the right side for fabrics knitted in fancy yarns, such as fur or eyelash yarn, as most of the textured effect of the yarn appears on the purl side of the fabric.

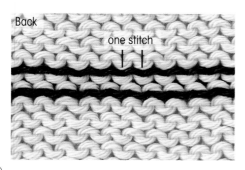

Back
one stitch

MAKING THE PURL STITCH

Each stitch is created with a four-step process. Hold the yarn at the front of the work – this is the side facing you.

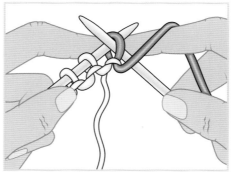

1 Place the needle with the cast-on stitches in your left hand, insert the right-hand needle into the front of the first stitch on the left-hand needle from right to left.

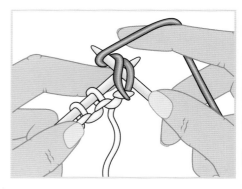

2 Take the yarn over and around the point of the right-hand needle.

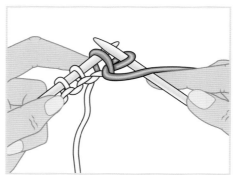

3 Draw the new loop on the right-hand needle through the stitch on the left-hand needle.

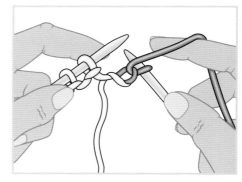

4 Slide the stitch off the left-hand needle. This has formed one purl stitch on the right-hand needle.

Repeat these four steps to the end of the row.

binding off (casting off)

Binding off (casting off) links stitches together so that they cannot unravel and secures stitches when a piece of knitting is complete. Binding off (casting off) is normally done following the stitch sequence, so a knit stitch is bound (cast) off knitwise and a purl stitch purlwise. It is important not to bind (cast) off too tightly; this may pull the fabric in and is a particular problem on a visible edge, such as on a mat or throw. If you find this is a problem, try using a needle a size larger than you use to knit the main fabric when you are binding off (casting off).

KNIT PERFECT

You will not be able to finish every project in one knitting session and will need to stop knitting and leave your work without binding off (casting off). Always complete a row – finishing in the middle of a row can cause your stitches to stretch or come off the needle. If you need to leave your knitting for a few weeks, make sure you have marked in the pattern where you have got to. If you are using stockinette (stocking) stitch, it may be a good idea to undo a few rows when you start knitting again. This will eliminate unsightly ridges that can be caused by stretched stitches – a danger when leaving your work on the needles for any length of time.

BIND OFF (CAST OFF) KNITWISE

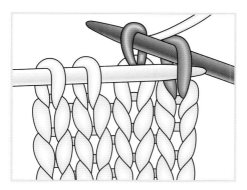

1 Knit the first two stitches. Insert the point of the left-hand needle into the front of the first stitch on the right-hand needle.

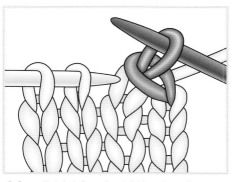

3 One stitch is left on the right-hand needle.

2 Lift the first stitch on the right-hand needle over the second stitch and off the needle.

4 Knit the next stitch on the left-hand needle, so there are again two stitches on the right-hand needle. Lift the first stitch on the right-hand needle over the second stitch, as in step 2. Repeat this process until one stitch is left on the right-hand needle. Cut the yarn and pass the end through the last stitch. Slip the stitch off the needle and pull the yarn end to tighten it.

BIND OFF (CAST OFF) PURLWISE

To bind off (cast off) a purl row, all you have to do is purl the stitches instead of knitting them.

BIND OFF (CAST OFF) IN PATTERN

When you are knitting in patterns such as rib or cables, it is important to bind off (cast off) in pattern to maintain an elastic edge. In this case, all that you have to do is knit the knit stitches and purl the purl stitches.

BIND OFF (CAST OFF) TOGETHER

This method, also known as the seam bind-off (cast-off), involves using a third knitting needle to join two pieces of knitting with the same number of stitches. The third knitting needle should be the same size as the needles used to knit the fabric, or one size smaller.

1 Place the two pieces of knitting that are to be joined right sides together and hold both needles in the left hand.

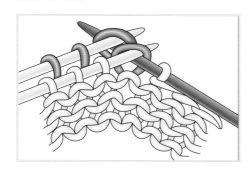

2 Insert the third needle into the first stitch on both the front and back needle and knit the stitches together. Repeat for the next two stitches.

3 Lift the first stitch on the right-hand needle over the second stitch and off the needle. Repeat the steps.

increasing stitches

Many projects are not square or rectangular and therefore need to be shaped by adding or removing stitches. This is called increasing and decreasing. There are several ways to do this and the ones you will need to make the patterns in this book are explained here.

MAKE 1 (M1)

This method allows you to create a new stitch in between two existing stitches that will be invisible. The increase may be described in your pattern as make one, abbreviated to M1.

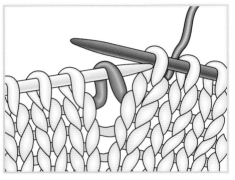

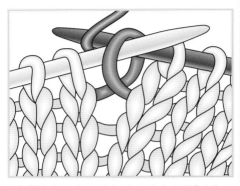

1 Work to the position of the increase and insert the left-hand needle under the horizontal strand between the next two stitches from front to back.

2 Knit this loop through the back to twist it. Twisting the stitch prevents a hole appearing and makes your increase practically invisible.

KNIT INTO FRONT AND BACK (KFB)

This method is most often used at the edges of the knitted piece. If done neatly, it is virtually invisible within the pattern of stitches. Make sure you keep an even tension as you add the stitches; when you are knitting into the same stitch twice, it is easy to make it very tight and therefore very difficult to knit.

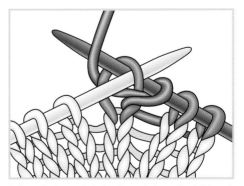

1 On a knit row knit the first stitch on the left-hand needle in the usual way, but instead of sliding the stitch off the left-hand needle as you would normally do, still keeping the yarn at the back of the work, knit into the back of the same stitch. Then slide the stitch off the left-hand needle. You now have two stitches on the right-hand needle and have therefore created a stitch.

2 On a purl row purl the first stitch on the left-hand needle in the usual way, but instead of sliding the stitch off the left-hand needle as you would normally do, still keeping the yarn at the front of the work, purl into the back of the same stitch. Then slide the stitch off the left-hand needle.

decreasing stitches

There are various methods of decreasing stitches that can create a pattern within the fabric, but this is the most straightforward method and it does not change the appearance of the knitted fabric apart from making it narrower. This decrease slants the fabric to the right.

k2tog

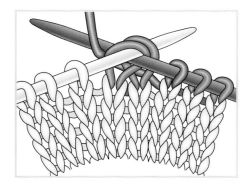

Knit to where the decrease is to be made, insert the right-hand needle knitwise through the next two stitches on the left-hand needle. Knit these two stitches together as if they were one stitch.

p2tog

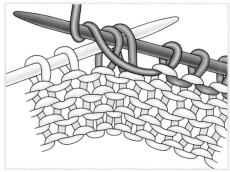

Purl to where the decrease is to be made, insert the right-hand needle purlwise through the next two stitches on the left-hand needle. Purl these two stitches together as if they were one stitch.

s1, k2tog, psso

This decrease slants the fabric to the left and decreases a stitch by using a slip one, knit one, pass slip stitch over technique; this binds the slip stitch around the knitted stitch, decreasing the row by one stitch. It is usually made a few stitches in from the beginning of a row. In patterns it can also be abbreviated to sk2po.

1 Knit to the position where the decrease is to be made. Insert the needle knitwise into the next stitch on the left-hand needle and slip it onto the right-hand needle without knitting it. Knit the next two stitches on the left-hand needle together.

2 Insert the left-hand needle into the front of the slipped stitch from left to right and lift it over the last stitch on the right-hand needle. This binds the slipped stitch around the last knit stitch and a stitch is decreased.

intarsia

In intarsia patterns separate areas of colour are worked within one knitted piece and each area of colour is worked with a separate ball of yarn. As you work, the yarns are twisted where they meet so the blocks of colour are held together. Intarsia is best worked over stockinette (stocking) stitch, although seed (moss) stitch and garter stitch are also effective. Intarsia patterns are worked from charts.

BOBBINS

When you knit with more than one colour of yarn, particularly for the intarsia method of colourwork, it helps to keep the yarns separate on bobbins to prevent them tangling and to make working easier. Hand-winding a small bobbin is quick and easy.

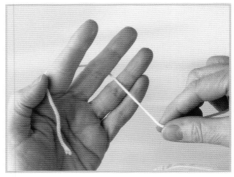

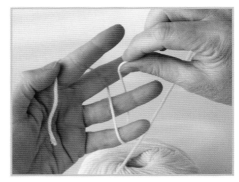

1 Place the end of the yarn from the main ball across your palm and hold in position with the thumb. Bring the yarn around the back of your forefinger and middle finger and then bring it to the front, towards your palm again.

2 Now take the yarn back in the opposite direction around the front of your ring finger and little finger and back through the centre again. This forms the first part of a figure-of-eight with the yarn around your fingers. Continue wrapping the yarn in this figure-of-eight configuration around your fingers.

3 Wrap until you have enough yarn for the bobbin around your fingers. Cut the yarn, leaving a tail that is approximately 8in (20cm) long.

4 Slip the yarn carefully off your fingers and hold the bobbin between the thumb and fingers of your left hand. Wind the yarn tail around the centre of the bobbin. Secure the tail by passing it under the last loop that you wrapped around the bobbin and pulling gently.

To use the bobbin, pull the unsecured end that started the bobbin, from the centre. Using this end of the yarn ensures that the bobbin does not tangle as you knit.

You can also buy plastic or card bobbins and wind the yarn around these instead of hand-winding. The technique is the same and it ensures that the yarn unwinds in the correct way to prevent tangling.

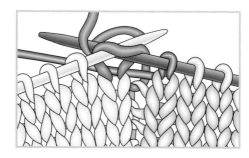

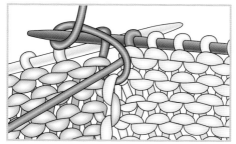

TWISTING YARNS ON A KNIT ROW

Work to the point where you need to change colour and insert the right-hand needle into the next stitch knitwise. Take the first colour over the top of the second colour. Drop the first colour and pick up the second colour, bring it up behind the old colour and continue knitting. The two yarns are twisted together. On the right side of the work there should be a smooth join between the colours.

TWISTING YARNS ON A PURL ROW

Work to the point where you need to change colour. Insert the right-hand needle into the next stitch purlwise. Take the first colour over the top of the second colour. Drop the first colour and pick up the second colour, bring it up behind the old colour and continue knitting. The two yarns are twisted together.

WORKING FROM CHARTS

Chart instructions for intarsia patterns can be produced as coloured squares or are printed in black and white with a symbol in each square representing the colour to be used. Each square of the chart represents one stitch and each line of squares represents one row. Rows that are worked on the right side of the fabric are read from right to left and are numbered up the side with odd numbers. Wrong-side rows are read from left to right and numbered up the side with even numbers. The exception to this is if you are working in the round on circular needles or double-pointed needles, when each round is read from right to left. Start knitting at the bottom right-hand corner of the chart at row 1. Unless otherwise stated, colour charts are worked in stockinette (stocking) stitch.

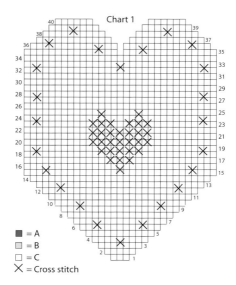

Chart 1

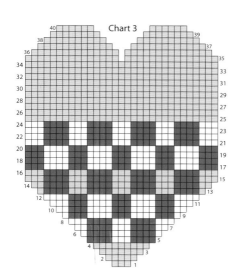

Chart 3

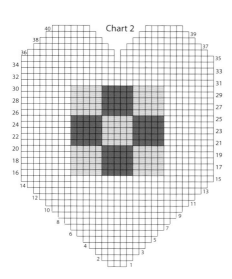

Chart 2

■ = A
■ = B
□ = C
✕ = Cross stitch

fair isle knitting

Fair Isle patterns use the stranding method to carry yarns across the back of the fabric. They are knitted in many colours, but there are never more than two colours in a row, which makes the stranding technique the perfect method for this style of colourwork. Fair Isle patterns are traditionally worked in stockinette (stocking) stitch. Like intarsia patterns, they are worked from a chart.

STRANDING

Stranding is used for small repeats of different colours worked across a maximum of four stitches. It is important that the loops of yarn between the different colours, called floats, are smooth and neat at the point the colour changes. To prevent the yarns twisting and tangling, one colour always lies above the other on the wrong side of the work. This allows the stitches on the front to lie flat and unpuckered and prevents holes between the colour changes.

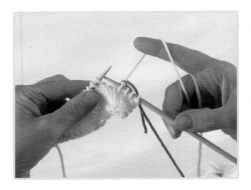

1 Knit to where you need to change colour. Drop the working yarn. Pick up the new yarn under the dropped yarn.

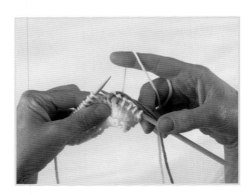

2 Knit the required number of stitches in this colour and then drop the yarn. Pick up the original yarn over the dropped yarn.

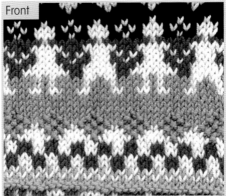
Front

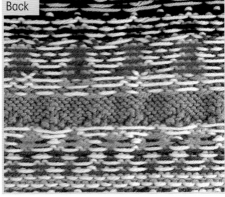
Back

3 Make sure that you stretch the stitches out on the needle slightly as you take the new yarn across the back of the stitches. This ensures that the loop of yarn at the back of the fabric is not too tight. On the right side blocks of colour should have an even tension.

WEAVING IN

When you have more than four stitches between colour changes you should weave the yarn not in use under and over the stitches until you use it again. If you leave loops of yarn that are longer than four stitches at the back of the fabric, they can catch and snag on your fingers or jewellery. Weave the yarn in every second or third stitch.

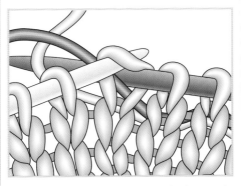

1 Work to the point where the second colour needs to be woven in. Insert the right-hand needle into the next stitch, bring the non-working yarn over the needle and wrap the working yarn around the needle as though to knit.

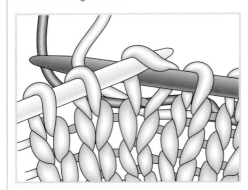

2 Pull the non-working yarn off the needle and finish knitting the stitch. The non-working yarn is caught into the knitted stitch.

Use the same technique on purl rows, bringing the non-working yarn over the needle before wrapping the working yarn to form the purl stitch, and then slipping the non-working yarn off the needle before completing the stitch.

cables

Cables are two sets of stitches that are twisted to form a rope. The cabling technique can also be used to carry stitches across the fabric. Placing stitches on a cable needle means that you can work sets of stitches on the same row in a different order. This is what creates the twisted rope effect of the cable. Placing the reserved stitches on a cable needle at the front of the work means that the cable will twist to the left. Placing them on the cable needle behind the work would twist the cable to the right.

C4F (CABLE FOUR FRONT)

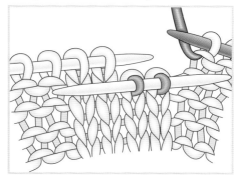 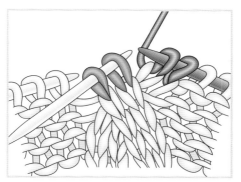

1 Slip the next two stitches from the left-hand needle onto a cable needle and hold it at the front of the work.

2 Knit the next two stitches on the left-hand needle in the usual way and then knit the two stitches from the cable needle. You can slip the two stitches back onto the left-hand needle and knit them from there if you prefer.

C4B (CABLE FOUR BACK)

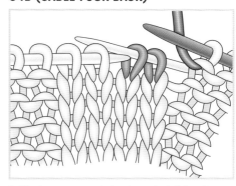 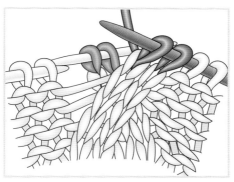

1 Slip the next two stitches from the left-hand needle onto a cable needle and hold it at the back of the work.

2 Knit the next two stitches on the left-hand needle in the usual way and then knit the two stitches from the cable needle.

C3F (CABLE THREE FRONT)
Work as C4F but slip one stitch onto the cable needle instead of two and hold at the front of the work, then knit two stitches.

C3B (CABLE THREE BACK)
Work as C4B but slip one stitch onto the cable needle instead of two and hold at the back of the work, then knit two stitches.

C8F (CABLE EIGHT FRONT)
Work as C4F but slip four stitches onto the cable needle instead of two and hold at the front of the work, then knit four stitches.

C8B (CABLE EIGHT BACK)
Work as C4F but slip four stitches onto the cable needle instead of two and hold at the back of the work, then knit four stitches.

circular knitting
(knitting in the round)

With circular knitting you work in rounds instead of rows; when you reach the end of a row, you simply carry on knitting without turning the work. This produces a tubular piece of fabric. Circular knitting can be made on either a circular needle or a set of double-pointed needles. Circular needles consist of two straight needles joined by a flexible plastic wire. They are available in sizes just like ordinary knitting needles and they also come in several lengths; the needles and connecting wire should be short enough so the stitches are not stretched when joined. Double-pointed needles are used for small tubular items such as gloves, hats and socks. They come in sets of four or five needles. You can cast on and knit whole items on circular needles or double-pointed needles, or use them to pick up stitches and knit a neck or a round shape, such as the sides of a basket.

WORKING WITH CIRCULAR NEEDLES

Cast on stitches as you would for ordinary knitting using a straight needle. Distribute the stitches evenly around the needles and wire, making sure they all lie in the same direction and are not twisted. The stitches should not be too far apart. If the stitches are stretched when the needles are joined, you need to use a shorter needle. The last cast-on stitch is the last stitch of a round. Place a marker here to indicate the end of the round and slip this on every round.

Hold the needle with the last cast-on stitch in your right hand and the needle with the first cast-on stitch in your left hand. Knit the first cast-on stitch, pulling up the yarn to avoid a gap between the stitches. Work until you reach the marker, checking that the stitches are eased around the needles as you work. This completes the first round. Continue knitting in this way for the required depth of the fabric tube.

CIRCULAR NEEDLES FOR FLAT KNITTING
Circular needles can also be used for knitting backwards and forwards in the normal way. This is especially useful where you have a large number of stitches, since the stitches will easily fit on the long needles and the weight of the fabric is held in front of you in your lap, rather than at the end of straight needles.

KNIT PERFECT
To remove any kinks from the nylon wire, immerse it in hot water for a few minutes and then gently straighten it.

WORKING WITH DOUBLE-POINTED NEEDLES

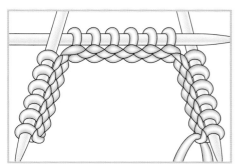

Using a set of four double-pointed needles cast onto one needle the total number of stitches required, then divide them evenly between three of the needles. The fourth needle is the working needle.

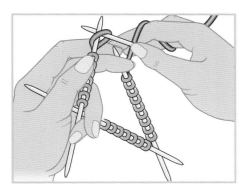

Arrange the three needles with the stitches into a triangle. The cast-on edge should face the centre of triangle; make sure it is not twisted. Place a marker here to indicate the end of the round and slip this on every round. Knit the first cast-on stitch, pulling up the yarn to avoid a gap between the first and third needle. Knit the remaining stitches from the first needle. The first needle is now empty and becomes the working needle.

Knit the stitches from the second needle onto the working needle. The second needle is now empty and becomes the working needle. Knit the stitches from the third needle onto the working needle. You have now completed one round. Continue working in this way to produce a piece of tubular fabric. Pull the yarn up as you switch between needles to avoid gaps at the changeover point.

KNIT PERFECT

Double-pointed needles also come in sets of five. The technique for using them is the same as for a set of four needles, only divide the stitches evenly over four needles instead of three, and use the fifth needle as your working needle.

Working the first round can be awkward; the needles not being used tend to dangle and get in the way. Don't worry – this will get easier once you have worked a few rounds and the emerging fabric helps to hold the needles in place.

fulling

Fulling is the process of turning a knitted fabric into an interlocked mass of fibres, which form a firm fabric that can be shaped and cut and will not fray. You can knit a specific item and then full it, or full an unwanted piece of knitted fabric and then cut it up and use it as you wish. The fabric is shrunk and turned into a dense mass of fibres by a combination of agitation, hot water and soap. The initial knitted fabric has to be pure wool, but even with this proviso some wool shrinks and fulls better than others. Merino wool is the preferred choice of professional fullers, but you may need to experiment to find wool that fulls well.

Fulling is often referred to as felting, although the two processes are different. The felting process is applied to carded unspun wool, while fulling is worked on a finished fabric.

HOW FULLING WORKS

Each wool fibre on an animal is covered with a protective membrane consisting of tiny scales that coat the fibre in the direction of the tip; this is to carry dirt and rain away from the body of the animal to the edges of its coat. These scales open and close to keep the animal warm in winter and cool in summer. Fulling takes advantage of these naturally occurring properties. Heat and moisture make the scales open up, so immersing the wool in hot water has this effect. Agitating the fibres makes them move closer together and shrink, and then placing the fibres in cold water locks this result and makes it permanent, producing a dense mass of fibres. Wool has a naturally neutral pH value and acidity or alkalinity has to be introduced to speed the process up. Soap has a high alkaline factor and it is hygienic, so it makes the perfect agent to use. Traditionally fulling is done by hand with the wool being rubbed by hand in warm soapy water and then being rolled backwards and forwards in a mat. However, this process happens automatically in a washing machine and this is an excellent way for the novice fuller to begin. Even though you cannot control the results as well as you can with hand fulling, it is still possible to produce some excellent fulled items.

CHECKING THE YARN

Before you start the process of fulling, there is a quick way to check whether the yarn you plan to use is suitable. It must be pure wool, but some wool has finishing agents added by the yarn manufacturers and this makes it less suitable. Take a small piece of yarn and add liquid soap to it. Wet it well with warm water, rub it and squeeze it in the palm of your hand to agitate the fibres. If the yarn is suitable, you will begin to see and feel the fibres matting together. Rinse the yarn by holding it under cold running water and squeeze out the excess moisture. The yarn should be more matted than when you started this process.

HAND FULLING

Always use laundry soap or soap flakes, not detergent or washing powder. Wearing gloves to protect your hands, dissolve the soap in hot water and immerse the item to be fulled. Knead the fabric without pulling, stretching or rubbing the knitting together. Check the fulling process frequently by removing the item from the water. Rinse the soap out of the item in cold water and pull it gently. If the stitches still move apart easily, you need to do more fulling, ensuring the temperature of the water stays hot. When the fabric is dense and fuzzy, rinse out the soap and squeeze out the excess water. Soak up extra moisture by rolling the item in a towel, and then lay it out flat to dry, away from direct heat.

It is advisable to try fulling out on samples of your fabric before fulling the completed item. Treat each sample differently, using hotter water or rinsing more often in cold water. Try to overwork one sample until it is matted and distorted to provide a comparison between correct fulling and matting. Keep notes of what you do and how long it takes as you go along. Then you will know the processes most likely to produce the desired result when fulling your item.

MACHINE FULLING

Wash several samples of your fabric with soap in a full load. If necessary, fill the machine with towels to add friction. Use the shortest hot/cold rinse cycle but do not spin. Remove the samples whenever possible during the cycle to check progress. You may need to run samples through the cycle more than once to achieve the desired effect. Always take out one sample at the end of each cycle as a record of the fulling process.

TEST SAMPLES

Here are three samples knitted in stockinette (stocking) stitch over the same number of stitches and rows. The first one (1) is not fulled, the second (2) is correctly fulled and the third (3) is distorted and matted rather than fulled.

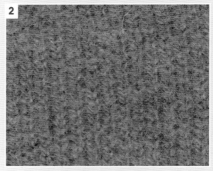

embroidery

Many of the projects in this book use simple embroidery stitches as embellishments. Why not try adding these to your other projects for a further touch of interest and glamour?

KNIT PERFECT

You can use embroidery thread, tapestry wool or knitting yarn, as long as it is the same or slightly thicker than the yarn used to knit the item. Check that the embroidery yarn is colourfast and has the same care instructions as the main yarn. Wash an embroidered sample if you are uncertain.

Always use a large-eyed blunt tapestry needle. To secure the embroidery yarn, weave it through a few stitches at the beginning and end of the embroidery, as knots may come undone during wear. Work your embroidery loosely; if it is too tight, it will make the fabric pucker.

SWISS DARNING

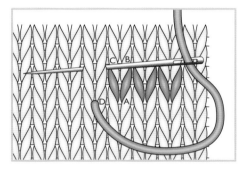

This stitch (also known as duplicate stitch) is used on stockinette (stocking) stitch to embroider small areas of colour that would be difficult or tiresome to knit. You could also use it to cover up any small errors made when knitting a colour pattern, as it looks as though it has been knitted into the fabric, although the stitches will appear slightly raised on the fabric surface. Always use the same thickness of yarn used in the knitted fabric.

horizontal stitches

Work from right to left. Bring the needle out at the base of the stitch (A). In one movement, take the needle under the two 'legs' of the stitch above the one to be covered (B) and then up at C. In one movement, take the needle down at the bottom of the stitch (A) and up at the bottom of the next stitch (D). Continue until the row of stitches is complete.

vertical stitches

Work from the bottom to the top. Work as for horizontal stitches, but instead of bringing the needle up at D, bring it up at the base of the stitch above the one just worked and continue up the line of knitted stitches.

CROSS STITCH

This is worked over one stitch and one row of stockinette (stocking) stitch. Ensure the top diagonal always goes in the same direction as the other cross stitches made.

Bring the needle up at A, down at B, up at C and down at D to make one stitch. When working a row of horizontal or vertical cross stitches, work one diagonal of each stitch to the end of the row, then work back putting in the other diagonal to complete the cross.

CHAIN STITCH

Bring the needle out at A. In one movement, put the needle back down in the same place and then bring it out at B for the next stitch, at the same time looping the thread under the needle.

LAZY DAISY STITCH

This consists of a series of detached chain stitches grouped together to form a pattern, usually a flower. Each chain stitch is fastened with a small stitch.

Bring the needle out at A. In one movement, put the needle back down in the same place and then bring it out at B for the next stitch, at the same time looping the thread under the needle. Take the needle down again at B, working over the loop. Bring the needle up at A to start the next stitch.

finishing techniques

The process of pinning and pressing knitted pieces is called blocking and it is important to make your finished garment looks as good as possible. Once you've spent all that time on your piece of knitting, it's worth the final effort to make it look really professional.

There are different methods for sewing your knitted pieces together. The methods used in the patterns in this book are explained here. Your pattern may suggest the best method for sewing up that particular project.

Another way to achieving a professional finish is to ensure that you pick up stitches evenly across the knitted piece when you need to knit an edging.

PICKING UP STITCHES

When you add a border to a piece of knitting, you pick up stitches evenly along the edge using one needle, usually a size smaller than that used for the main fabric. Hold the work in your left hand with the right side facing you. Insert the needle through the edge stitches, wrap the yarn from a new ball around the needle and pull the loop through.

on a horizontal bound off (cast off) edge
Holding the work in your left hand with the right side facing you, insert the needle into the centre of the first stitch in the row below the bound off (cast off) edge. Wrap the yarn knitwise around the needle and pull the loop through. Continue in this way until the required number of stitches have been picked up.

on a vertical edge
Holding the work in your left hand with the right side facing you, insert the needle between the first and second stitches at the beginning of the first row. Wrap the yarn knitwise around the needle and pull the loop through. Continue along the edge, inserting the needle between each row, until the required number of stitches have been picked up. To reduce bulk if using thick yarn, insert the needle through the centre of the edge stitch, therefore taking in only half a stitch.

SEWING UP

If possible, sew up your items with the same yarn you used to knit them. If the yarn is very thick, highly textured or breaks easily, use a plain yarn in a matching colour. Use a tapestry needle and keep the length of the yarn you use to sew up at reasonable lengths, so it does not fray as it continually passes through the fabric: 18in (45cm) lengths are most suitable.

MATTRESS STITCH

Use mattress stitch to produce an almost invisible seam. This stitch is worked from the right side of the fabric, allowing you to match patterns and shaping details.

joining two pieces of stockinette (stocking) stitch

Lay the pieces to be joined out flat, right sides up and together. Secure the pieces together by bringing the needle through from back to front at the bottom of the right-hand piece, taking the needle through the left-hand piece from back to front and back under the right-hand piece and out at the front. This makes a figure-of-eight with the yarn and gives a nice start to the seam.

Take the needle across and under the left-hand piece and bring it through to the front from the same hole as the securing stitch. Now take the needle back to the right-hand piece and bring it up under the horizontal strands of the two stitches above the first entry point. Take the needle back to the left-hand piece, insert the needle back into the stitch that the yarn is emerging from and take the needle up under the next two horizontal strands. Pull up the stitches to tighten them and draw the two edges together. Continue working from side to side in this way, tightening the yarn every few stitches but not so tight as to pucker the fabric.

joining two pieces of reverse stockinette (stocking) stitch

Work as for joining two pieces of stockinette (stocking) stitch, but take the needle under only one horizontal strand of the knitting. On the first row, take the needle under the horizontal strand of the row above. Take the needle across to the other piece of knitting and take it under the top loop of the second stitch above. One side of the seam takes in one and a half stitches and the other takes in one stitch, but this process weaves the rev st st together, making the seam invisible.

BACKSTITCH

This is worked from the wrong side of the fabric and is used when you require a strong seam, but don't have to match the stitches row for row. The way the pieces are joined creates a seam allowance, which can be bulky, so you should sew your seam as close to the edge of the pieces as possible. Backstitch is often used to seam cushions and join different pieces of knitted fabric.

Place the pieces to be joined, right sides together and pin in place. Bring the needle through from the back to the front, one knitted stitch down from the starting edge. Insert the needle one knitted stitch back and bring it out one knitted stitch ahead. Pull the yarn through to tighten and form a stitch. Repeat this step as you continue along the seam, making one backstitch cover one knitted stitch.

SLIPSTITCH

Using slipstitch to join a band or collar to the main piece of knitting means that you can work from the right side and check that the pieces are easing and fitting together properly as you work. On stockinette (stocking) stitch garments, the bands or collars are often worked in garter stitch or seed (moss) stitch, so the stitches will not match to the main piece, but the overall length should.

1 Place the pieces to be joined together, right side up, and check that the piece to be attached is the correct length. You may have to stretch it very slightly to make the pieces fit perfectly. Pin the pieces together, if necessary. Bring the needle through from the back on the main piece, taking the needle under the horizontal bar of the first stitch.

2 Take the needle across the front to the edge of the band and pick up the horizontal bar in the corresponding stitch. Take the needle back to the main fabric and bring it up through the next stitch from back to front, again taking the needle under the horizontal bar.

3 Bring the needle under the horizontal bar of the corresponding stitch on the band. Gently tighten the yarn to bring the edges of the two pieces together. Continue working up the seam in this way. Tighten the yarn every few stitches to pull the edges together as you work to allow the stitches to lie flat with no puckering.

OVERCASTING

Overcasting creates a narrow seam that is also flat, so it is a useful method of joining knitted pieces. It is usually worked from the wrong side, but it can also be worked from the right side in a contrasting yarn to create a decorative finish. In this case you have to be careful to space the stitches evenly.

Pin the pieces to be joined with their right sides together, matching the stitches exactly. Join the yarn securely at the edge of the two seams. Work along the seam taking the needle under the strands at the edge of the seam, between the matched 'bumps', from back to front. After each stitch, tighten the yarn gently over the knitted edge. Keep the tension of each stitch the same. The join between the two pieces should be neat and flat with no bulky ridge.

DOUBLE CROCHET SEAM

This is a technique for joining two bound-off (cast-off) edges of stockinette (stocking) stitch together. It is worked on the right side of the fabric and makes a raised seam. Place the pieces to be joined together with wrong sides facing. Double crochet stitch can also be used to add a decorative edging to a piece of knitting.

1 Insert the crochet hook into the inside loop of a bound-off (cast-off) stitch on each piece. Catch the yarn and pull a loop through.

2 Insert the hook into the inside of the next two bound-off (cast-off) stitches and pull through a loop. There will be two loops on the hook. Catch the yarn and pull it through both these loops on the hook to complete one stitch. Repeat steps 1 and 2 to complete the seam.

3 The finished seam will have a raised join along the right side, which is a decorative feature.

STEAM PRESSING

This method is used for natural yarns or those with a high wool content. Yarns with a high synthetic content will not stand the high temperatures of steam pressing, and care should be taken with long-haired fibres such as mohair and angora and items with textured stitches to ensure the fibres are not matted or the pattern flattened by the steaming process. Always check the information on the ball band before pressing and test out how your fabric will react on your gauge (tension) square first if you have any doubts.

Use rustproof large-headed pins to pin out each piece to its exact measurements, wrong side up, on your ironing board or blocking board. You can make your own board from a large piece of chip board or similar material covered with a layer of foam and then a layer of checked or gingham fabric. This will give you lines to guide you when pinning out your knitting. Staple the fabric to the reverse of the board. Lay a clean cotton cloth over your knitting to protect it.

Set the iron to an appropriate heat setting for your yarn. Hold the iron close to the surface of the knitting and allow the steam to permeate. Do not press the iron onto the knitted fabric. Remove the cloth and allow your knitting to dry thoroughly before unpinning.

WET PRESSING

This alternative method is suitable for synthetics and fancy yarns. Pin out your knitting to the exact measurements on your ironing or pressing board as before. Wet a clean cloth and squeeze out the excess water until it is just damp. Place the cloth over your knitting and leave to dry. Remove the cloth when it is completely dry and ensure the knitted pieces are also dry before unpinning them.

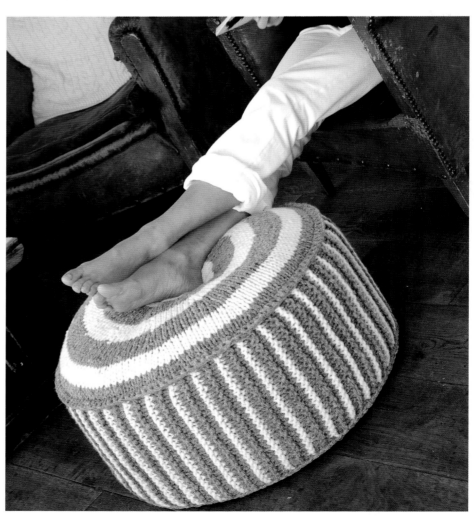

embellishments

Here are instructions for some simple embellishments that may be just the finishing touch you need to turn your item into something really special.

TWISTED CORD

You can twist strands of yarn together to form a cord. The more strands used, the thicker the cord will be. Cut lengths of yarn that are three times the finished length required and knot them together at each end. Hook one end over a hook, doorknob or other convenient place and hold the other knotted end so that the strands are held taut. Put a pencil in this end and wind it in a clockwise direction to twist the yarn. Remove the end from the doorknob and bring the knotted ends together, allowing the cord to twist around itself. Hang a weight on the yarn to keeping it taut, or ask someone to hold it taut for you. Knot the other end to secure.

I-CORD

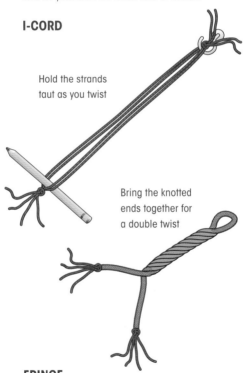

Hold the strands taut as you twist

Bring the knotted ends together for a double twist

FRINGE

Wrap the yarn loosely around a piece of cardboard that is the length of the fringe required. Cut along the yarn at the bottom edge and remove the cardboard. Fold several lengths in half and use a crochet hook to pull the loop of strands through the edge of the knitting from front to back. Thread the ends of the strands through this loop and pull to tighten. Each bunch of yarn should be evenly spaced along the edge. Trim the ends of the fringe to the required length if necessary.

An I-cord is a knitted tube that can be used as a tie, as a cord through a drawstring opening, as a border or even as a fake cable decoration. You can thread piping cord through the knitted tube to make it firmer if you want to use the cord to edge a cushion or make handles. They are easy, although a little time-consuming, to make. They are usually made with knit stitches and are worked on two double-pointed needles that should be two sizes smaller than the needles normally used for the yarn. An I-cord is usually worked from four stitches, or you can use three stitches for a finer cord and five stitches for a thicker one. More than five stitches is not recommended.

Cast four stitches onto one of the needles in the usual way. Knit one row, do not turn the work but instead push the stitches to the other end of the needle. Swap right-hand and left-hand needles, bring the yarn across the back of the stitches and pull it up tightly. Knit the four stitches again and repeat this process for every row. Working in this way will produce a tubular piece of knitting.

POMPOM

Cut two circles of thick cardboard that are slightly larger than the diameter of the finished pompom. Cut a circle from the centre of each circle half this size. Wind yarn around the circles until the centre hole is filled. Carefully cut through all the loops of yarn around the edge of the circle and then gently ease the discs apart so there is a straight section of yarn visible between them. Take a small piece of yarn and tie it firmly around the middle of the pompom, knotting it as tightly as possible. Ease the circles off the pompom and fluff it up into a round shape. Trim around the pompom, turning it as you work, to give an even shape, leaving the two yarn ends for securing to your knitting.

troubleshooting

Don't worry – all knitters make a mistake sometimes. Here are some of the more common mistakes made and instructions on how to correct them.

DROPPED STITCHES

Dropped stitches have fallen off the needle and unravelled down, creating a ladder effect in the fabric. This is easily rectified if you notice it quickly, so take time to check your knitting every few rows. If you do not notice until you have completed a lot more knitting, the only solution will be to unravel your work back to the point of the dropped stitch. If you try to pick it up, you will create an area of tight stitches, as the ladder left by the dropped stitch will have closed up and there will be no spare yarn to use to create the extra stitch.

knit stitch dropped one row below

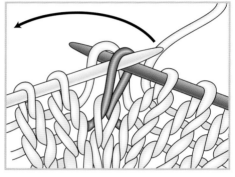

Make sure that the horizontal strand of yarn is behind the dropped stitch. Insert the right-hand needle into the dropped stitch from front to back and under the horizontal strand of yarn behind it. Insert the left-hand needle into the dropped stitch and lift the stitch over the horizontal strand and off the right-hand needle.

stitch dropped several rows below

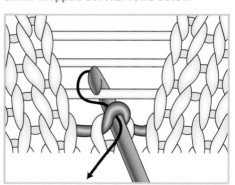

purl stitch dropped one row below

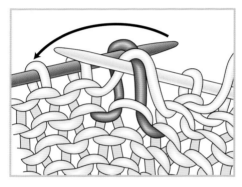

Make sure that the horizontal strand of yarn is in front of the dropped stitch. Insert the right-hand needle into the dropped stitch from the back and under the horizontal strand of yarn in front of it. Insert the left-hand needle into the dropped stitch and lift the stitch over the horizontal strand and off the right-hand needle.

To pick up a knit stitch, insert a crochet hook through the front of the stitch, catch the yarn strand immediately above and pull it through the stitch. Repeat for all strands in the ladder up to the top of the knitting and slip the stitch back onto the left-hand needle.

To pick up a purl stitch, follow the instructions for a knit stitch but work from the wrong side of the fabric.

UNRAVELLING ONE ROW

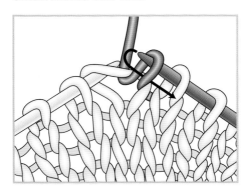

Unravel the knitting stitch by stitch back to the error. With the front of the fabric facing you, put the left-hand needle into the stitch below the stitch on the right-hand needle, drop the stitch off the right-hand needle and pull the yarn. Repeat this for each stitch until you reach the error. Purl stitches are unravelled in the same way.

UNRAVELLING SEVERAL ROWS

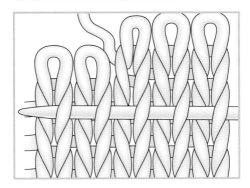

Find the row that you want to take your knitting back to, which should be just below the error. With the right side of the fabric facing you, take a knitting needle that is smaller than the needles you are working with and weave it in and out of each stitch on the row. Work from right to left across the whole row, passing the needle under the right-hand and over the left-hand sides of the stitch.

Remove the original needle from the top of the fabric. Gently pull the yarn away from the stitches and they will unravel, one by one. Continue in this way until you reach the smaller needle. Transfer the stitches on this needle to a needle of the correct size, making sure that you do not twist the stitches in this process, and continue knitting.

SPLIT YARN

When you are working fast, it can be easy to split a strand of yarn or to miss a strand when using several strands together. Always unravel and rework the stitch, otherwise it will be visible on the finished fabric.

INCOMPLETE STITCHES

This can happen if you wrap the yarn around the needle but do not pull it through the old stitch to form a new one. You can work the stitch properly following the instructions for how to deal with dropped stitches.

CABLES

If you notice that you have twisted a cable the wrong way before you knit the next twist, you can unravel and reknit the stitches involved. If the mistake is some way down your work, you will need to unravel completely to that point and reknit your piece again to avoid problems with stitch gauge (tension).

SNAGGED STITCHES

Use a tapestry needle to ease the extra yarn back through any distorted stitches, one by one, beginning with the stitch closest to the snagged area.

RUNNING OUT OF YARN

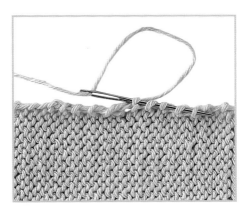

Always aim to join in new balls of yarn at the beginning of a row or at a seam edge, so that you will be able to weave in the yarn ends neatly. Drop the old yarn and knit the next few stitches with the new yarn. Tie the ends at the beginning of the row together securely so the ends do not slip out and unravel your work. When you have finished knitting, undo the knot and weave one end up the edge of the fabric for a few inches, doubling back for a few stitches to secure it. Do not pull too tightly and distort the fabric. Weave the other end in the opposite direction in the same way.

To estimate how much yarn you have left when coming to the end of a ball, lay your knitting flat and measure the remaining yarn four times across the width of the knitting. This would be sufficient yarn to work another row of stockinette (stocking) stitch, but textured and cable patterns would need more. It is always best to start a new ball if in doubt, to avoid running out of yarn in the middle of a row and having to unravel your knitting.

aftercare

Looking after your hand-knitted items is almost as important as knitting them accurately! It is always best to be ultra-cautious when washing them because there is nothing worse than ruining something that has taken so many hours of hard work.

KNITTING NOTEBOOK

You may like to keep a ball band and a small sample of the yarn used in each project in a notebook. The ball band will give specific care instructions, as different types of yarn require different treatments. Always look out for yarns that are dry clean only.

WASHING

Knitted items can be washed either by hand or machine according to the instructions on the ball band. Hand washing will always give you more control over the washing process than machine washing.

To hand wash, prepare the item by closing any zips or openings and doing up the buttons. This will help to keep the shape of the item. Also remove any non-washable trims or buttons – these should come with their own care instructions. Use soap flakes, mild detergent or specially formulated hand wash liquid; do not use biological washing powder as this is too harsh. Use hot water to completely dissolve the detergent and then leave the water to cool to lukewarm. Add the knitted item and lay it flat in the water. Gently press it up and down with your hands to work the soap through the item; do not rub or twist the knitting.

RINSING

Rinse the item in lukewarm water, again pressing the fabric rather than squeezing or wringing it. The water should run clear after the final rinse. Keep the washing process as short as possible. Gently press out the excess water. Remove the knitted item from the sink or bowl using both hands to support it. You want to avoid the weight of the water still in the fabric dragging the item out of shape.

DRYING

Knitted items should be dried as quickly as possible. If they are left damp for too long, they can mildew and develop a musty smell. Lay the item flat on a large towel and roll up the towel. This squeezes the excess moisture into the towel. You can repeat this several times, changing the towel as necessary. You can also wrap the knitted item in a towel and put it in the washing machine and spin on a short cycle. To finish the drying process, lay the item on a dry towel and reshape it, smoothing out the fabric. Leave it to dry in a warm place but away from direct sunlight. You can turn the item several times during the drying process. Machine drying is not a good idea for hand knits, but you can fluff up mohair by placing it in a dryer on a cool setting for a minute or two after it is completely dry.

MACHINE WASHING

Follow the washing instructions on the ball band carefully and never wash an item made from yarn that only gives instructions for hand washing. Use a delicates or wool cycle with a short spin. Lay flat to dry.

STORING KNITTING

Knitted items are best stored in clean fabric bags to protect them from dust. Fabric bags are better than plastic as they allow the air to circulate. Plastic bags can make natural fibres sweat and become damp. You can put a moth-repellent into any bags containing wool items. It is a good idea to air your stored knitted items outside before wearing.

KNIT PERFECT

The most common disaster after washing is the garment shrinking and fulling. This results in an item that is smaller, hard and matted and is beyond salvation. The three reasons why this happens are friction, agitation and heat. This is why you should never machine wash a yarn that only gives instructions for hand washing. It is not just a question of temperature; the agitation of the spin cycle alone can be enough to damage the fibres in the yarn.

If a yarn can be machine-washed, it will say so clearly on the ball band. If in doubt how to wash your knitted item, wash the gauge (tension) swatch and see how it reacts, before attempting to wash your knitted item.

suppliers

Except where stated in the patterns, the specific yarns used to make the projects in this book have not been listed as yarn companies frequently discontinue colours or ranges and replace them with new yarns. You should have no trouble finding a suitable yarn by referring to the information given in the yarn descriptions for each pattern. A guide on substituting is given below, together with contact details for some of the major yarn spinners around the world.

SUBSTITUTING YARNS

This is how to work out how much of a particular yarn you need for each project.

1 The number of balls of yarn × the number of yards/metres per ball given in the pattern = A

2 The number of yards/metres per ball of the yarn you wish to use = B

3 A ÷ B = number of balls required in the yarn of your choice.

Art Yarns
www.artyarns.com
(USA) Art Yarns
39 Westmoreland Avenue
White Plains, NY 10606
Tel: +1 914 428 0333
(UK) Get Knitted
39 Brislington Hill, Brislington
Bristol BS4 5BE
Tel: +44 (0)117 941 2600
www.getknitted.com
(AUS) Ristal Threads
PO Box 134, Mitchell,
Canberra 2620
Tel: +61 (0)2 6241 2293
www.ristalthreads.com
email: info@ristalthreads.com

Colinette
www.colinette.co.uk
(USA) Unique Kolours
28 North Bacton Hill Road
Malvern, PA 19355
Tel: +1 800 252 3934
www.uniquekolours.com
email: uniquekolo@aol.com
(UK) Colinette Yarns Ltd
Banwy Workshops
Llanfair Caereinion SY21 0SG
Tel: +44 (0)1938 810128
email: feedback@colinette.com

Crystal Palace Yarns
www.straw.com
(USA) Crystal Palace Yarns
160 23rd Street, Richmond
CA 94804
(UK) Hantex Ltd
Whitehouse Yard, Eaudyke
Friskney, Boston, Lincs
PE22 8NL
Tel: +44 (0)1754 820800
www.hantex.co.uk/
email: sales@hantex.co.uk

Debbie Bliss
www.debbieblissonline.com
(USA) Knitting Fever Inc.
315 Bayview Avenue, Amityville
NY 11701
Tel: +1 516 546 3600
www.knittingfever.com
email: admin@knittingfever.com
(UK) Designer Yarns Ltd
Units 8–10 Newbridge
Industrial Estate
Pitt Street, Keighley
West Yorkshire BD21 4PQ
Tel: +44 (0)1535 664222
www.designeryarns.co.uk.com
email: enquiries@designeryarns.uk.com
(AUS) Prestige Yarns Pty Ltd
PO Box 39, Bulli, NSW 2516
Tel: +61 (0)2 4285 6669
www.prestigeyarns.com
email: info@prestigeyarns.com

Jo Sharp
www.josharp.com.au
(USA) JCA Inc.
35 Scales Lane, Townsend
MA 01469
www.jcacrafts.com
Tel: +1 978 597 8794
(AUS) Jo Sharp Hand Knitting Yarns
PO Box 357, Albany, WA 6331
Tel: +61 (0)8 9405 8207
email: yarn@josharp.com.au

Kaalund
www.kaalundyarns.com.au
(USA) Jumbuck Fibers
San Juan, Capistrano
California
Tel: +1 949 481 6696
email: donnaandaus@aol.com

(UK) Kangaroo
Knights Court, Bevernbridge
South Chailey BN8 4QF
Tel: +44 (0)1273 400030
www.kangaroo.uk.com
(AUS) Kaalund Yarns Pty Ltd
PO Box 17, Banyo, Qld 4014
Tel: +61 (0)7 3267 6266
email: yarns@kaalundyarns.com.au

Louisa Harding
www.louisaharding.co.uk
(USA) EuroYarns
315 Bayview Avenue
Amityville, NY 11701
Tel: +1 516 546 3600
www.euroyarns.com
(UK) Designer Yarns Ltd
Units 8–10 Newbridge
Industrial Estate
Pitt Street, Keighley
West Yorkshire BD21 4PQ
Tel: +44 (0)1535 664222
www.designeryarns.co.uk.com
email: enquiries@designeryarns.uk.com
(AUS) Prestige Yarns Pty Ltd
PO Box 39, Bulli, NSW 2516
Tel: +61 (0)2 4285 6669
www.prestigeyarns.com
email: info@prestigeyarns.com

Noro
www.eisakunoro.com
(USA) Knitting Fever Inc.
315 Bayview Avenue
Amityville, NY 11701
Tel: +1 516 546 3600
www.knittingfever.com
(UK) Designer Yarns Ltd
Units 8–10 Newbridge
Industrial Estate
Pitt Street, Keighley
West Yorkshire BD21 4PQ
Tel: +44 (0)1535 664222
www.designeryarns.co.uk.com
email: enquiries@designeryarns.uk.com
(AUS) Prestige Yarns Pty Ltd
PO Box 39, Bulli, NSW 2516
Tel: +61 (0)2 4285 6669
www.prestigeyarns.com
email: info@prestigeyarns.com

Patons
www.coatscrafts.co.uk
(USA/CAN) 320 Livingstone Avenue South
Listowel, ON, N4W 3H3
Canada
Tel: +1 888 368 8401
www.patonsyarns.com
email: inquire@patonsyarns.com
(UK) Coats Crafts UK
PO Box 22, Lingfield House
Lingfield Point, McMullen Road
Darlington DL1 1YJ
Tel: +44 (0)1325 394237
www.coatscrafts.co.uk
email: consumer.ccuk@coats.com
(AUS) Patons
PO Box 7276, Melbourne
Victoria 3004
Tel: +61 (0)3 9380 3888
www.patons.biz
email: enquiries@auspinners.com.au

Rowan
www.knitrowan.com
(USA) Westminster Fibers Inc
165 Ledge Street, Nashua
New Hampshire 03060
Tel: +1 603 886 5041/5043
www.westminsterfibers.com
email: info@westminsterfibers.com
(UK) Rowan
Green Lane Mill, Holmfirth
HD9 2DX
Tel: +44 (0)1484 681881
email: info@knitrowan.com
(AUS) Australian Country Spinners Pty Ltd
Level 7, 409 St Kilda Road
Melbourne, Victoria 3004
Tel: +61 (0)3 9380 3888
email: tkohut@auspinners.com.au

Sirdar
www.sirdar.co.uk
(USA) Knitting Fever Inc.
315 Bayview Avenue
Amityville, NY 11701
Tel: +1 516 546 3600
www.knittingfever.com

(UK) Sirdar Spinning Ltd
Flanshaw Lane, Alvethorpe
Wakefield WF2 9ND
Tel: +44 (0)1924 371501
email: enquiries@sirdar.co.uk
(AUS) Creative Images
PO Box 106
Hastings, Victoria 3915
Tel: +61 (0)3 5979 1555
email: creative@peninsula.starway.net.au

South West Trading Company
www.soysilk.com
(USA) See website for stockists
(UK) Create & Knit
The Old Granary Studios
Priory Nurseries
Breedon on the Hill
Derbyshire, DE73 8AT
Tel: +44 (0)7594 437948
www.createandknit.co.uk
(AUS) See website for stockists

Sublime
www.sublimeyarns.com
(USA) Knitting Fever Inc
PO Box 336, 315 Bayview Ave
Amityville, NY 11701
Tel: +1 516 546 3600
www.knittingfever.com
email: admin@knittingfever.com
(UK) Sublime Yarns
Flanshaw Lane
Wakefield
West Yorkshire
WF2 9ND
Tel: +44 (0)1924 369666
email: contactus@sublimeyarns.com
(AUS) Creative Images
PO Box 106
Hastings, Victoria 3915
Tel: +61 (0)3 5979 1555
email: creative@peninsula.starway.net.au

Twilleys
www.twilleys.co.uk
(UK) Twilleys of Stamford
Roman Mill, Stamford PE9 1BG
Tel: +44 (0)1780 752661
email: twilleys@tbramsden.co.uk

index